D0984346

The Anthropology of Sibling Relations

The Anthropology of Sibling Relations

Shared Parentage, Experience, and Exchange

Edited by Erdmute Alber, Cati Coe, and Tatjana Thelen

First published in 2013 by PALGRAVE MACMILLAN® in the United States—a division of St. Martin's Press LLC, 175 Fifth Avenue, New York, NY 10010.

Where this book is distributed in the UK, Europe and the rest of the world, this is by Palgrave Macmillan, a division of Macmillan Publishers Limited, registered in England, company number 785998, of Houndmills, Basingstoke, Hampshire RG21 6XS.

Palgrave Macmillan is the global academic imprint of the above companies and has companies and representatives throughout the world.

Palgrave® and Macmillan® are registered trademarks in the United States, the United Kingdom, Europe and other countries.

ISBN: 978-1-137-33122-9

Library of Congress Cataloging-in-Publication Data

The anthropology of sibling relations: shared parentage, experience, and exchange / edited by Erdmute Alber, Cati Coe and Tatjana Thelen.
    pages cm
    ISBN 978-1-137-33122-9 (alk. paper)
    1. Brothers and sisters. 2. Brothers and sisters—Family relationships.
3. Social adjustment in children. 4. Ethnology. I. Alber, Erdmute.

HQ759.96.A57 2013
306.875'3—dc23   2013002339

A catalogue record of the book is available from the British Library.

Design by Scribe Inc.

First edition: July 2013

10 9 8 7 6 5 4 3 2 1

To Claudia Roth, our colleague and friend,
who passed away much too early in July 2012.

CONTENTS

Figures

ACKNOWLEDGMENTS

How a book comes into existence is always a long story to tell. The initial conception of this volume happened in a conversation between Erdmute Alber and Sjaak van der Geest in 2007, when we realized how important sibling relations were for understanding social relations and talked about their neglect in social anthropology. This led to the organization of two workshops: one at the biannual conference of the European Association of Social Anthropologists in 2008 in Ljubljana and a second one in 2009 at Thurnau castle, near Bayreuth, financed by the Bayreuth International Graduate School of African Studies (BIGSAS) of Bayreuth University. The first meeting served as a kind of brainstorming about siblingship in light of new kinship studies; first drafts of all the chapters in our book were presented at the second. We give thanks to BIGSAS and its coordinator, Christine Scherer, for funding, as well as to Julia Brix for organisational support of the second workshop. Furthermore, we thank all the participants of the workshop for their intellectual spirit in discussing the drafts of the papers, particularly Janet Carsten and David Sabean. During the Thurnau meeting, Cati Coe and Tatjana Thelen joined Erdmute Alber in the project, but our special thanks go to Sjaak for having put the idea of a new book on sibling relations on the agenda.

The editing process of this book would have been much more complicated without the technical support of Jakob Treige and Heike Schwankl. Thanks to both!

We note with sadness that one of the participants, our dear colleague Claudia Roth from the University of Luzerne, passed away in July 2012. Like the siblings introduced in the following pages, she shared in our key (intellectual) experiences and provided social support in times of uncertainty. Her research on gender, intergenerational relations, age, and social security in Burkina Faso added greatly to our discussions around siblingship, kinship, and intergenerational care over the years. We wish we could have continued this exchange over many more years, perhaps even by reading her review of this book, rather than dedicating it to her memory.

CHAPTER 1

THE ANTHROPOLOGY OF
SIBLING RELATIONS
EXPLORATIONS IN SHARED PARENTAGE,
EXPERIENCE, AND EXCHANGE

Tatjana Thelen, Cati Coe, and Erdmute Alber

Since the 1990s, after a gap following David Schneider's critique (1984), there has been a remarkable revival of kinship in anthropology. The new kinship studies shifted interest to practices, processes, and meanings in contrast to a previous focus on jural rights and obligations, kin terms, and structures. Within this efflorescence of the literature, certain issues have dominated, while others have been largely overlooked. Exciting issues entailing moral and legal dilemmas or contesting biological notions of kinship dominate the research agenda. These include reproductive technologies (Rapp 1999, Franklin and Ragoné 1998), international adoption and the constructions and surrogates of parenthood (Howell 2006, Leinaweaver 2008, Marre and Briggs 2009, Stryker 2010, Yngvesson 2010), and "new" legally recognised forms of alliance (Smith 2001, Weston 1991). Their common ground is to highlight how kinship is produced through social practices rather than determined by the physical act of birth.

However, the "new" kinship studies have something in common with "classical" anthropological research on kinship: much of the scholarship generated by the new approach has remained within the frame of what was formerly called, in the older kinship literature, alliance and descent. In contrast to the multifaceted discussions around biological as well as social parenting ("descent") on the one hand, and marriage and other forms of connecting and disconnecting couples on the other ("alliance"), other relations within the *web of kinship*, as Meyer Fortes (1949) called it, remain largely neglected. One of these neglected themes is the relations between brothers and sisters—the theme of our book. We argue that these relations are as important to the maintenance of families and households as parenthood and marriage.[1] Thus a focus on siblingship, we argue, not only puts a largely neglected relation at the center of attention but allows us to revise the "old" problem of social cohesion.

Linked to this first issue, our second point is that putting sibling relations at the center allows for insights into the making and breaking of kinship ties across the life course. Michael Lambek (2011) and Tatjana Thelen (2010) point out that the recent literature on kinship focuses on the first stages of life rather than other forms of kinship that may be more significant later in life and that involve separation, alliance, and changing forms of exchange and reciprocity. Siblingship gives us an opportunity to explore how relatedness is created, maintained, and broken over the entire life course and even thereafter. It constitutes a unique entry point into questions of flexibility and stability, as people creatively enact their cultural understandings of kinship roles in changing circumstances. This is so, among other reasons, because relations between siblings do not start inevitably at the moment of birth, nor even during childhood. As the papers by Erdmute Alber and Cati Coe in this volume show, people may discover or mobilize sisters or brothers during different phases in their life cycle and for different purposes; moreover, the actual behavior as well as the role expectations of siblings may change over time. And finally, as Lambek (2011) argues, looking at kinship from the perspective of the end of life makes the relations of siblings even more important. Succession frequently depends not only on the parent-child relations but also on the (mutual) acceptance of siblings.

Furthermore, the diversity of sibling relations involving different genders, generations, and norms makes it an extremely fruitful field for looking at how meaningful relations are generated and maintained in various contexts. In the West, with its emphasis on the centrality of parent-child and conjugal relations, "the rules for conducting a sibling relationship have never been established; ambivalence is its keynote, and instability its underlying condition" (Sanders 2002: 1).

Although in other contexts, like in South Asia, sibling relationships across the life course are more strongly defined and articulated (Weisner 1993), even there, there is variability in the emotional intensity and level of conflict that specific siblings experience. Siblingship seems to be established and maintained through diverse means. Brothers and sisters may be defined by their common biological fathers or mothers, such as through being the children of the same sperm donor (Sabean 2009). However, shared childhoods may be as significant as shared parenthood in establishing the feelings associated with siblings—whether warmth and affection, or jealousy and rivalry. Through shared experiences in households where they are fostered, the children of siblings or even nonkin can grow attached to one another and call one another sisters and brothers, as the paper by Julia Pauli shows. Furthermore, as adults, providing economic support can be a significant part of the relation, including raising or supporting siblings' children, as discussed by Helena Obendiek and Erdmute Alber. These norms can vary during different life phases of siblings and be brought to bear differently at different points in the life course. For example, economic and social support, or a sense of intimacy, between adult siblings may be mobilized on the basis of mutual suffering during a shared childhood (Pauli) or on the basis of shared parentage despite not knowing one another, whether at all or well, in childhood (Alber).

Some of the reason for the diversity of norms, other than that they may change across the life course, is because siblings are constructed simultaneously as equal or similar (as children of the same parents) *and* as different, because of their differences in birth order, age, and gender status. A. R. Radcliffe-Brown posited that siblings were equivalent to one another generationally (we discuss his ideas further in the next section), and sibling relations do entail relations between people of more or less the same age. However, they also entail relations between older and younger siblings, between sisters and brothers, and between adult siblings with different social class positions, economic and social capital, and connections through marriage. In both their similarity and diversity, sibling relations are modeled on other relations and simultaneously provide models for other kinship relations. For instance, the "motherly care" of an older sister toward her younger sibling builds on conceptions of parenting, but it does not make the relation a parent-child bond, yet the relation is also different from a sibling relation that builds on shared suffering in the past. Similarly, "equality" or closeness as a norm in sibling relations might be the basis for the ideal marriage or friendship, as Sjaak van der Geest discusses. We do not fully develop this theme in this volume, but it is important to keep in mind that calling somebody "brother" in order to express solidarity is a very frequent expression of closeness in many regions of the world (Dent 2007; see also Baumann 1995 on "cousins"). Furthermore, imaginaries of brotherhood and sisterhood have been used to mobilize social movements and provide a sense of intimacy to the abstract concept of the nation (Herzfeld 2007) and to community life within religious orders (Hüwelmeier 2009).

The diversity not only of forms but also of norms might be a reason that the analytic exploration of siblingship has been hampered. The contributions in this volume take the opposite perspective, however: they show that it is exactly this variety that provides insights into the creating, maintaining, and breaking of meaningful relations. Because of its inherent variety, siblingship proves to be a privileged entry point to revisit "old" questions regarding the relation between friendship and kinship, intimacies conceptualized as incest, and forms of support across social class, generation, and geographic distance. In the following pages, we give a short overview on the scattered reflections on siblingship within anthropology, followed by a tentative systematization of the three ways siblingship is therein conceived, before proceeding to the contributions of the collected papers.

Siblings: Back to Beginnings

There is a remarkable silence around siblingship in anthropology, not only compared to the amount of literature on other kin relations, but also given the significance placed on sibling relations in many other popular and scientific discourses.[2] Moreover, the existing anthropological literature on the complex relation between brothers and sisters does not form a unified body but seems to be scattered among the literatures on kinship and socialization.[3] Some attention was given to siblingship in classic kinship anthropological works, but there have been different regional traditions in doing so, leading to different insights and gaps. This section does not attempt to give a comprehensive overview of the anthropological literature on siblingship, nor does it deal with the many empirical case studies. Rather, we summarize some central theoretical arguments about siblingship and their underlying reasoning. As with so many themes in the anthropology of kinship, we return to the structural-functional "classics" as the fathers—not *parents*, as mothers are largely missing—of anthropological thinking about siblingship. Like Michael Herzfeld (2007) in his discussion of global kinship, we return to these classical works reflexively, in the spirit of mining them for what is useful.

As far as we can see, the first theorem was formulated by Radcliffe-Brown, who already in 1924 was thinking about the prominent position of the mother's brother in South Africa (Radcliffe-Brown 1924). Interestingly, the debates about the central position of the mother's brother that started with this essay and continued in the kinship literature rarely examined the cross-gender sibling relation between the "mother" and her "brother." Rather, a way of thinking about the intergenerational effects of siblingship was invented, without examining the sibling relation itself. An underlying rationale for this thinking was the orientation toward descent theory within structural functionalism and its interest in social cohesion through kinship. A key question has been how far the special position and ambivalent authority of the mother's brother toward the children of his sister expressed an old and still underlying matrilinearity or whether the extent of the relation between the mother's brother and the sister's son confirmed the relations between children and their matrilateral descent group within a general setting of patrilineality (Radcliff-Brown 1924, Goody 1959; for a review of the debate see Bloch and Sperber 2004). Although structural-functionalist studies aimed at explaining social cohesion, they failed to see the contribution of the interaction between the mother's brother and his sister, including the role played by the children in creating and sustaining a relation between the adult siblings.

The second contribution of Radcliffe-Brown to the study of siblingship is his notion of the "principle of the unity of the sibling group" (1950), which is connected to what he names the "principle of the equivalence of siblings" (1971). What he meant by this is that siblings are mutually substitutable, because they all hold the same position in the kinship structure. This perspective comes from a way of thinking about kinship that is oriented around descent and descent alone. It tends to oversee the vast differences in the position of siblings—a point to which we return later.

The structural conception of marriage, which soon was to challenge descent as the dominant organizing principle of kinship in anthropological thinking, was characterized by a similar omission in theorizing sibling relations. Claude Lévi-Strauss, for instance, in his work on the structures of kinship (1969) perceived the exchange of women, through marriage, to be a form of communication between two groups of brothers. How these brothers specifically interacted with their sisters who were given in marriage was not considered interesting. One reason for the neglect of the sibling relation was that structuralists saw the core family (and the incest taboo in particular) as the basis of other social relations. Thus, besides marriage, all other kinds of cross-gender relations between women and men were not of particular interest in kinship theory (see Weiner 1992 for a similar argument). Marriage was viewed as the exchange par excellence on which other forms of exchange were modeled, so that women were seen mainly as wives, rather than as sisters, who enabled their brothers' marriages through the exchange of bride price.

With the symbolic and later postmodern turn, yet another focus on siblings and the basis of their relations became central. Following David Schneider, Mac Marshall was most explicit in emphasizing that siblingship is a cultural category with a specific meaning used for "full" as well as for "half" or "fictive" brothers. In view of the Polynesian material, he rejected descent-oriented thinking, which viewed classificatory naming as first used for "full consanguines" and then extended to other, like relations (Marshall 1983: 2). In contrast, he argued in favor of a notion of siblingship that takes different practices of co-residence or created kinship into account. Thereby he put stress on what Schneider had called "the code of conduct": "To act *like* siblings is to *become* siblings" (1977: 649; emphasis in original). Contributing to more than a sense of diversity, Marshall's research pointed to the importance of mundane practices of nurturing as well as feelings of closeness in establishing and maintaining meaningful ties. The interest in processes of making kin was later expanded within what became known as "new kinship." For example, Mary Weismantel (1995) in her study on Zumbagua adoption in the highlands of Ecuador showed the importance of feeding practices for establishing parenthood. Similarly, Janet Carsten's work (1997) on the making of kinship among the Malay highlights the central role that processes of sharing food play.

Although presented here in chronological order, all three ways of constructing and understanding siblingship are still salient in theory as well as practice. In the next section, we explore these different ways of constructing siblingship, as each highlights different aspects and constraints of a possible relation, before turning to the ways siblings are seen as a model of and for other relations.

THREE WAYS OF CONSTRUCTING SIBLINGSHIP

In line with the proposition put forward by Mac Marshall in 1977 in relation to kinship in general, we formulate the three different defining criteria of siblingship as different modes of sharing. First, siblingship as shared parenthood focuses attention on the wider ramifications of the sibling relationship, particularly intergenerationally. Second, the construction of siblingship as based in shared experience highlights siblings' childhoods and similarity. Finally, siblingship through the lens of exchange and care facilitates a longitudinal perspective and highlights the differences between siblings, particularly as adults.

Siblings through Shared Parentage— Highlighting Intergenerational Significance

As noted, in the structural-functional paradigm, relations between siblings are perceived as deriving from shared parentage: Radcliffe-Brown understands a sibling group to be "the body of brothers and sisters of common parentage" (1950: 24).[4] Common descent from the same parents often entails sharing intergenerational obligations such as managing care for aging parents, calling the same people with the same kinship term, and being jointly involved in legal cases of inheritance, among others. These characteristics make the sibling relation unique. Shared parentage could be extended to social siblings; it could be plural or exclusive; but, in any case, it would remain parentage.[5] Sharing parents can give siblings a sense of similarity and connection.

However, that siblings share parents—be it shared mothers, fathers, or both—does not necessarily mean that they experience equivalence in relation to their parents, which is the second part of Radcliffe-Brown's formulation. The principle of the unity of the sibling group has been criticized, among other reasons, for not emphasizing the importance of the seniority principle. Seniority can, for example, be expressed by different kinship terms, as it is in the case in many African languages (Van der Geest, this volume). In Baatonum, the language of the Baatombu Alber writes about in this volume, for instance, the older brother or sister is called by a different kinship term than the younger brother or sister. Additionally, sharing parents can result in sibling rivalry or tension, which is a prominent theme in Western culture; the Bible is full of violent sibling rivalry (Schwartz 1997). The psychodynamics within families means that siblings tend to react to one another in responding to situations, such as taking on the roles of "the good child" and "the bad child." The siblings of a terminally ill child may put on a front that they are fine to prevent a parent from worrying about them, because their ill sibling is causing such anxiety and concern within the family (Bluebond-Langner 1991). The topic is highlighted particularly well in the psychological literature (Adler 1924, Sutton-Smith and Rosenberg 1970, Sanders 2009), and rivalry appears not only in childhood but also later in life, especially in issues around succession, inheritance, and caring for elderly parents (Hohkamp 2011; Lambek 2011; Gluckman, Mitchell, and Barnes 1949; Van Vleet 2008).

Even though it is easy to reject the idea of the unity of the sibling group as well as the principle of equivalence of siblings based on the empirical evidence, nevertheless we think that Radcliffe-Brown's concept is valuable in grasping at least one aspect of sibling relations. When boys or men call themselves brothers in order to emphasize their mutuality, equality, and closeness, they are mobilizing the concept of sibling unity for social purposes. The same happens, of course, in the case of girls or women who call themselves sisters in order to express their closeness. In addition, closeness and mutuality are also constructed between brothers and their sisters, as various European fairy tales, such as "Hansel and Gretel," prove. Moreover, the conceptualization of siblingship as shared parenthood by Radcliffe-Brown and others gives us the sense that sibling relations are significant in creating and sustaining ties across the generations. As Igor Kopytoff points out, siblingship is not solely an intragenerational connection.

The early insight gained from the discussion of the role of the mother's brother toward his nephews and nieces has to be extended, however, to the relationship between the father's sister and her respective nieces or nephews, as Alber discusses in her paper, and to the brother's sister in relation to her brother's children (Meier 1999). The same holds true for the no-less important relations between children and their father's brother, who is, especially in settings characterized by patrilineality and patrilocality, frequently named a father himself (see Müller 1997). In patrilineal and patrilocal settings where brothers live together with their wives and their respective children, the children of brothers often call themselves brothers and sisters as well. This fact is nevertheless due to the relationship between brothers, their descent from the same parents, and its effect on the next generation. And of course, the relations between sisters—often overlooked in the literature—are equally essential for their children. Heike Drotbohm (2012), for example, discusses a case of sisters who mutually care for their children in the context of transnational migration.

Furthermore, siblings play a key role in creating kin ties in the next generation when they foster one another's children or maintain their relationships by giving gifts to one another's children. In South India, the mother's brother's gifts to his sister's daughters at ritual occasions were viewed as the sister's share of her parents' inheritance maintained by her brother (Kapadia 1995). As Obendiek's paper shows, a wealthier sibling may support a poorer sibling by educating his or her children, so that those children can support their parents in the future. Siblingship can therefore even continue after a sibling's death, as it constructs aunt/uncle-nephew/niece relations. Sibling relations can also affect the previous generation of parents. For example, Coe found in her research that southern Ghanaians worry that the conflict between step-siblings will cause divorce among new couples, and they therefore prefer to have children from previous marriages live with grandparents, aunts, or uncles.

Shared parentage is one way that siblingship is constructed and understood. As a perspective, it highlights the ways that sibling relations affect relationships across the generations. In contrast, in the second way of conceptualizing siblings—on the basis of shared experience—the emphasis is more on feelings of mutuality.

Siblings through Shared Experience:
Creating Feelings of Similarity

Sharing parents is not the only way to see oneself as a sibling, nor does it automatically lead to feelings of being close to a sibling. Shared experiences during childhood can also result in people calling themselves brothers or sisters. This point is particularly highlighted in Pauli's paper, which shows that children related by more distant blood ties may "choose" to become (and stay) siblings because they share distinctive childhood memories. Having experienced a common childhood and shared food, suffering, and joy gives siblings a sense of similarity that, seemingly, reflects the structural equivalence argument. However, the basis of such a relation is not—as Radcliffe-Brown would probably have it—their being born into that position; instead, their shared experience generates feelings of similarity that can be converted into practices of mutuality.

Demographic changes over the last hundred years have resulted in shared childhoods becoming even more important in Western families and elsewhere. In earlier times in Europe, poverty, inheritance rules, and educational rules among peasant and artisan households caused some siblings to leave the house around age fourteen. Younger siblings might be born after an older sibling had departed from the household, and some of the intervening siblings may not have survived their early childhood (on changing demographic and kinship patterns in Europe, see for example the contributions in Grandits and Heady 2003 and Grandits 2010). Similarly, in southern Ghana, where having eight to ten children was normal in the mid-twentieth century, the older siblings were perhaps ten to fifteen years older than their younger siblings and could help raise them, taking some of the burden of the younger siblings' school tuition from aged parents. Now that parents can usually expect to see all their children grow up, in Ghana and elsewhere, they have fewer children more closely spaced and therefore more similar in age. These fewer children grow up with more shared experiences and can expect more long-lasting relations. This changes the quality, content, and construction of these relations.

However, even when siblings grow up together, they may in fact grow up in different environments because there is different investment in siblings because of their gender, birth order, health, or personality (Johnson and Sabean 2011); families may be at different stages in the life course, with fewer or greater resources (Weisner 1993); and larger social and political changes create different schooling and economic conditions for children of different ages (Obendiek, this volume). In seventeenth-century German court society, siblings were dispersed among courts across Germany, sometimes to the care of their aunts and uncles at those courts, so that they did not share childhoods with one another but rather with their cousins and the children of the destination court (Ruppel 2011).

Gender is a major differentiating factor: relations between brothers and sisters are often perceived and lived out differently than those between brothers or those between sisters. Evelyn Blackwood (2005) and Barbara Meier (1999) have pointed out that classic kinship studies have highlighted the roles of women as mothers and wives, but not as sisters, despite the significance of the latter role in giving women (and often their brothers) economic and social status (Gluckman, Mitchell, and Barnes 1949; Weiner 1992; Pauli, this volume). Wives may even be sisters to one another, as in sororal polygamy. Opposite-sex siblings may be more reserved with one another (Kipp 1986), or they may be freed from the rivalries that plague same-sex sibling relationships, as Van der Geest's chapter suggests. Opposite-sex siblings may socialize one another to become gendered, sexualized persons prior to marriage. In Lebanon, for example, "through the brother/sister relationship, men learned that loving women entailed controlling them and women learned that loving men entailed submitting to them" (Joseph 1994: 56; see also Melhuus 1996). Davidoff (2011) demonstrates how opposite-sex sibling relations in families in nineteenth-century Britain were central in constructing a concept of the self through simultaneous identifying and distancing from the other. On the basis of these reflections, it might be more useful to discuss how similarity is not a given but rather constructed between siblings through actively created experiences.

This insight brings us back to the notion of similarity—but now on the basis of shared experience, rather than shared parentage—that also seems to be the basis of an imagined ideal type of siblingship. Although we acknowledge the significance of similarity in idealizations of sibling relations, we want to underline the fact that shared experience does not always lead to similarity, as illustrated particularly well in Pauli's paper. The ways in which siblings may care for one another through different phases of the life course, despite their different social positioning, is the third way of constructing lasting relations identified in the literature we examined.

Siblings through Exchange and Care: Living Difference and Mutuality

While, as noted before, Lévi-Strauss (1969) saw the exchange of women as a dominant form of exchange between two groups of brothers, Marshall (1977) was one of the pioneers in describing the importance of daily practices of nurturing in establishing kinship relations. Thus, finally, siblings can be conceptualised through their exchanges and mutual caring obligations. For example, on the Trobiand Islands, sisters serve their brothers cooked food even after marriage, and their brothers are responsible for making them large yam gardens (Weiner 1992: 75). These reciprocal exchanges and acts of care create and sustain kinship relations. Sometimes the exchange is of material goods like food and cloth. In other cases, the exchanges are based on emotional labor, such as care, support for education, fostering one another's children, mutual support in marriage crises, or caring in old life.

Whereas shared childhoods draw attention to similarity of experience—even if only ideologically—the focus on practices of exchange and mutual care draws attention to the differences between siblings. Although we may assume that similarity engenders closeness, in fact hierarchy and difference may also elicit feelings of closeness. Older and younger siblings may develop strong ties through dependency and care: the older siblings may have been teachers in joint play activities or the child-minders of the younger siblings, carrying them around on their backs or in a sling (Kipp 1986; Rabain-Jamin, Maynard, and Greenfield 2003). Alexander Dent (2007) describes how the harmonic resonance between Brazilian male singing duos is built on hierarchy and difference around the older brother / younger brother roles, which also affects other social aspects of the brotherly duos' relationships.

Siblings may have very different trajectories and life histories, taking on different kinds of work and marrying partners of differing wealth, status, and cultural and political capital (Johnson and Sabean 2011: 3). They may end up in different socioeconomic classes, as described in Pauli's case study of two Mexican sisters. It is because of their differences that siblings can help one another, as Coe's paper discusses—whether sisters their brothers, older siblings their younger siblings, or richer siblings their poorer siblings. As Obendiek's paper shows, siblings' different social and economic capital enables a sibling's support and care for another (or for that sibling's children). Siblings can even affect one another's trajectories through others' assumptions that care and exchange flows between siblings. For instance, a young man who migrates from Morocco to Spain increases the marital prospects of his sister—in terms of the number and status of her suitors and the size of her bridewealth—because it is assumed that her in-laws may even obtain access to Spain through the brother-sister relation (Empez Vidal 2011).

In our work on sibling relations, we find the focus on exchange and care particularly important among adult siblings, as sibling relations develop and change across the life course. As Alber's paper shows, such acts of support can establish sibling relations where none existed before. However, it is important to note that siblings are affected by their differences in ways that do not always lead to exchange and care between them. Different socioeconomic trajectories between siblings can result in mutual support, with some resentment, as we see in Obendiek's paper, or envy and rivalry, as we see in Pauli's paper. Siblings may collaborate or compete within families for access to resources, which becomes especially obvious in routes to succession. One can also "lose" siblings through the lack of exchange and care: Van der Geest's paper shows how sibling relations can sour when a sister takes sides with her husband rather than her brother. (Similarly, a sister may grow closer to her brother following a divorce; Niehaus 1994.) A sister in fifteenth-century Germany who failed to serve as a link to another house through her marriage—as an agent of power and alliance between her brother and her husband's families—could be cast aside (Hohkamp 2011). Sibling relationships can worsen at the moment of succession, at the point of the parents' deaths, in complex and unpredictable ways (Lambek 2011) or become closer as siblings coordinate their elderly parents' care.

The previously outlined three modes of establishing and maintaining siblingship—through shared parenthood, experience, and exchange/care—are, in turn, linked to different ways siblings are seen as a model of and for other relations, which will be explored in the next section.

Siblings as a Model of and for Other Relationships

In 1965, psychological anthropologist Francis L. K. Hsu put forward a controversial hypothesis. He argued that different societies had different dominant dyads—whether father-son as in China, husband-wife as in America, or brother-brother as in some African societies (note again the omission of sister relations). The characteristics of these dominant dyads "tended to determine the attitudes and action patterns that the individual in such a system develops towards other dyads in the system as well as towards his relationships outside the system" (Hsu 1971, 10). This theory was widely criticized: how does one determine which relationship is dominant—are they jurally or emotionally significant? Are dyads more important than larger groupings like lineages or triads? Do particular dyads like brother-brother dyads have intrinsic universal attributes? What are the psychological and interpersonal mechanisms by which the dominant dyad affects other relationships? Like the anthropologists Ruth Benedict and Margaret Mead, Hsu seemed to be trying to explain an entire society through an essential pattern—in this case a single type of relationship. Although we agree with the critiques, we think Hsu raises an important point about the cultural variation in the ideological significance of various relationships, and how ideologically and psychologically salient relationships can serve as models for other social relations, as the different regional literatures on siblingship reveal. Siblingship derives much of its centrality for wider social organisation from the way it is used as an ideal or metaphor for other relations.

However, we do not conceive of siblingship as having universal attributes that define the societies in which it is the dominant or model relation. Instead, the different ways of constructing siblingship as based on shared parentage, experience, or exchange/care raise the question of how people themselves think about sibling relationships. We have already mentioned the issue of naming. It is not only people who share biological mothers or fathers who call themselves brothers or sisters but also other men and women as a sign of solidarity. As noted before, it is quite normal for sons and daughters of brothers in patrilineal or of sisters in matrilineal settings to call themselves brothers and sisters. Like words in a language (de Saussure 1983), siblingship exists in symbolic relation to other terms for relationships, defined not by its reference to a fixed object but by people's inter-subjective participation in one another's lives (Sahlins 2011, 2010). Close friends may call themselves brothers or sisters in order to give emphasis to the closeness of their relation. These terms for relation-ships are defined partly by what they are not, through comparisons and contrasts with other terms for relationship.

Within the different regional literatures, the other relations that siblingship serves as a model of and for vary. For example, in contrast to the way that Africanists perceived siblingship as a relation of minor importance in comparison with descent, many scholars of Oceania and Southeast Asia put siblingship in a central place. Among the Samo, Marshall (1983: 9) describes, siblingship becomes the principle for hamlet organization. In an even broader sense, Janet Carsten argues that in the Malay fishing community where she works the majority of social relations are modeled on siblingship. It is siblingship that encapsulates the most central meanings of kinship morality, and a set of siblings seems to be the basis of every house (Carsten 1997: 82ff.).[6] Because siblings are not considered divisible among the Malay, sepa-rating siblings seems to be a problem for parents, even if fosterage is also quite common in the region. Carsten deals here not only with "real" lived sibling relations but also with the imaginary of siblingship as a model for social relations in general.

Because of the significance of sibling relationships in Southeast Asia and Oceania, siblingship becomes the important point of comparison and contrast with marriage. If in many African settings, marriage is viewed as a completely different relation than siblingship, Carsten and Margaret Trawick, working in South Asia (1990), describe how mar-riage can be modeled after an ideal of harmonious siblingship. Rita Smith Kipp (1986) describes how Karo Batak lovers may use sibling terms in their endearments, suggesting that the love between siblings is the model for love between lovers or marital partners, transforming a chosen relation into one that is given—one of kin. Thomas Gibson (1995), working in Ara, Sulawesi, describes marriage itself as a pro-cess of ritually transforming spouses into siblings. And Marie Reay (1975–76: 80) argued that the Kuma value sisters over wives and see a brother-and-sister pair as two halves of a whole.

Siblingship and marriage can also overlap. Shirley Lindenbaum, in her overview of ideologies of masculinity and femininity in Papua

New Guinea societies (1987), mentions that in small, so-called homosexual societies, ideally a married sister and her brother share a sexual partner. Much ritual attention is also paid to separate brothers and sisters, thereby making brothers the sole possessors of their paternal substance. Thus, rather than the incest taboo, it is the fusion of brothers and sisters and their treatment as one person that seems to constitute a problem and makes a differentiation of cross-sex siblings necessary (Lindenbaum 1987: 229–30; see also Godelier 1986 on Baruya men who prefer to marry a woman from their own lineage, technically a sister).

Similar to the centrality of siblingship in southeast-Asian mythologies, the Abrahamic religions share Genesis as a myth of origin in which we have reason to believe that the patriarch Abraham is married to his half-sister Sarah with whom he shares the same father (Delaney 2001). This emphasis on siblingship is connected to a privileging of brother-sister relations that can be found in the anthropological literature on the Middle East. Some authors posit that brothers are the instrument of patriarchal control over women, while others have emphasized that opposite-sex sibling relations are characterized by mutual love not found in other family relationships (Joseph 1994). For example, Hilma Granqvist, in a study of Palestinian peasants in the 1930s, asserted that the love between brother and sister was more beautiful than that between husband and wife: "The husband is only a garment which a woman puts on or throws off again, or she herself can be 'thrown off' by the husband, but the brother is one who is always there" (quoted in Joseph 1994: 52).

Because of siblingship's adjacent relationships (Demian 2004), the relationships with which they are compared and contrasted, some sibling relationships are more culturally marked than others. The marriage-siblingship analogy privileges the brother-sister relationship and the complementary roles of brother/sister and husband/wife, whereas descent-oriented thinking highlights siblings of the same sex for their equivalence and substitutability, as in the studies of African lineage brothers. As a result, whereas the Africanist and Europeanist literature tends to neglect the brother-sister relation, the southeast/ south Asian and Middle East literature illuminates the close bond between brother and sister, stronger than marriage, and tends to overlook same-sex sibling relations. These differences mean not only that there is not one notion of siblingship in the world but, perhaps more important, that sibling relations have to be seen and understood in the context of other kinship relations—marriage being one of them. Insights can come from focusing on less culturally marked sibling relations as well as more prominent ones, as Alber shows in her paper (see also Sofue 1971).

While different definitions of siblings can be at play simultaneously in people's lives, with different aspects emphasized at different stages of the life course, states are also involved in imagining, defining, and regulating siblingship, thus affecting sibling relations as lived. Because the state's effect on kinship relations has hitherto been mostly researched in regards to parent-child relations and marriage (for example Bushin 2011 and Griffiths 1997), in the next section we pay special attention to the state and discuss in greater depth the most significant ways in which it impacts siblings. As with the other topics discussed, we see siblingship as a privileged entry point for grasping the interplay between the state and kinship in general.

SIBLINGS, POLITICS, AND THE STATE

Overlooking siblingship as an important relation can have serious consequences for the analysis of political relations and social inequalities. First, the sense of the nation as an intimate body politic is often constructed on ideal versions of siblingship (Herzfeld 1997). Second, the underestimated role of sisters for their brothers' social position can lead to a mistaken picture of hierarchies and politics in a given society. Sibling relations have far-reaching consequences for the succession of power, possession, and knowledge. For example, in the Samoan case, the close relation of a sacred sister to her brother secures power and authority for both of them (Weiner 1992: 80). Finally, it may lead to neglecting the role of state policies in creating and defining sibling relations and vice versa. Four kinds of state policy, we argue, have the most effect on sibling relationships: state education systems; state laws that affect birth planning and spacing as well as constructions of shared parenthood; inheritance law; and finally the construction of the nation on the basis of ideologies of siblingship, which among others affect immigration laws.

Schools and state education systems influence sibling relationships in a variety of ways. While schools are associated with children, they can influence siblings not only in childhood but throughout the life course. For instance, siblings may acquire different educational credentials and thus different employment opportunities, as Pauli's case study of the Namibian sisters shows. Alber's chapter discusses the effects of a girl's being excluded from further schooling and the support her brother—a university student—can provide. Education and employment may create a middle class with new views of sibling relations, as Coe's chapter examines in Ghana. Shifts in educational policies can also create different kinds of opportunities in different generations, causing shifts in lived sibling relations, as Obendiek shows in her diachronic perspective on sibling sets in China. Furthermore, the expansion of schooling and educational credentialing worldwide over the course of the twentieth century raised the degree of investment required for children to be economically and socially successful—to be fully grown "adults" (as the literature on youth in Africa would have it). This development has had a number of effects on parent-child relationships and expectations of reciprocity between the generations, such as the greater significance paid to fathers and the resources they could provide to children (Allman and Tashjian 2000) or the degree to which children's obligations to provide elder care to parents were dependent on the parent's investment in the child's education and success in life (Aboderin 2004, Alber 2012). A failed pay-off of investment into education may also lead to a reversing of obligations toward care for the elderly, as Roth (forthcoming) shows in the example of *badenya* (siblings sharing a mother) in urban Burkina Faso. Furthermore, because parents do not always have the resources to meet their educational obligations to their children, they turn to their own siblings or to their more successful children to help them with this responsibility, as Obendiek's and Coe's chapters show in China and Ghana, respectively, creating complex and long-term reciprocities between siblings between and within the generations.

These processes can also affect the ways children are exchanged between siblings. As Jamila Bargach (2001) relates, her own adoption was interpreted as a sacrifice made by her mother for her sister who had no daughter. In contrast, when around thirty years later Bargach's sister offered her daughter to Bargach in structurally the same procedure, it was taken as a sacrifice for the future of the girl, who could receive better schooling in the United States. Schooling, with its long-term expected payoffs in terms of employment, seems to have contributed to siblings (as well as parents and children) thinking about their reciprocal exchanges in more long-term ways. Finally, because older children are now expected to go to school, they have less time to help with child minding, thus placing more of a burden on adults to care for small children and reducing siblings' significance in child socialization (Schildkrout 1978). Juliet Mitchell (2003) relates a news story that the state of Kerala, in southern India, had announced an extension of child- and baby-care services—not, as she expected, to help their mothers work, but to encourage their older sisters to go to school.

State polices and state laws also affect relations between siblings through their influence on demographic trends. In general, worldwide developments are toward lower fertility rates and a decrease in the number of siblings, while newer reproductive technologies are also increasing the rate of twins and multiple births. State policies aiming at decreasing or increasing birth rates influence these tendencies and the use of technologies. The most dramatic case is China's one-child policy, which has resulted in an absence of siblings through singleton births in urban areas and a reduction in the number of siblings in rural areas very quickly in the space of one generation. This has led singleton children to experience increased pressure to become members of the elite, with heavy parental investment in their educations and high expectations to take care of their elders (Fong 2004), rather than responsibility and support spread among a group of siblings like in the more rural families described in Obendiek's paper. State policies in other countries, by placing the burden for raising children on families, such as by not subsidizing or providing early childhood education, encourage a small family size and a small sibling set. States also can enable or hinder access to contraception and abortion services (on such pronatal politics in socialist Romania, see Kligman 1992).

In addition to influencing demographic trends, and thus the number of people who consider themselves brothers and sisters, state laws constitute an important apparatus framing the relations between siblings. Even in twenty-first-century Europe, state laws oblige parents to take some financial responsibility for their adult children in case they fail economically. The siblings of these adult "failures" may be affected by their parents' financial transfers. Furthermore, as in India, adult children may be legally obligated to support their elderly parents (Lamb 2009). In situations where their parents have no resources, brothers and sisters may cooperate in caring for their parents (Roth forthcoming), which in some cases creates sibling conflicts in addition to a means of cohesion on the basis of mutual interest.

Maybe of even more importance, inheritance law creates siblings, as brothers and sisters commonly inherit their parents' goods. State law in its capacity of an enforceable norm is decisive for maintaining particular rules und definitions concerning sibling relations. Today we witness a privileging of shared (biological) parenthood over other constructions in many states. For example, in Germany, up to thirty years ago, inheritance laws privileged children born within wedlock in contrast to those who were born in extra-marital relations. These laws created different classes of siblings. With the revoking of this law, new problems and distribution conflicts emerge in what are today called patchwork families. It becomes clear that the law in such instances follows, although often belatedly, the changing norms of lived kinship experience. Always contested, enforcing specific norms can become more conflictual or painful in situations of cross-cutting legal orders and migration.

Whatever rights immigrants have to be with their families is predicated on idealized conceptions of families in the host country. States establish legal definitions of what a sibling is, and they tend to rely on notions of shared parentage rather than basing it on shared childhoods, feelings of intimacy, or reciprocal exchanges. Especially in countries where national identity is modeled on shared blood or family, the incorporation of those defined as others or outsiders is problematic. In the United States, siblings are defined genetically, through a DNA test, and legalistically, through contracts and legal papers governing the transfer of legal rights, rather than through childhoods shared through informal fosterage practices or as children of siblings (cousins). Because of American ideals that adults establish independent households with a spouse and children, adult siblings are considered less important and are low on the priority list for family reunification in US immigration law. Furthermore, state immigration policies can have a profound effect on sibling relationships, because they are not well coordinated with the strategies of those who migrate. For example, most Ghanaian immigrants bring over their families in a stepwise fashion, rather than immigrating as a family unit, whether because of difficulties of immigrating legally or because of the costs associated with immigration. A man may migrate alone, and then bring his wife, and finally their children may join them. In the meantime, the parents may have had more children. Birth order—in relation to a parent's migration—can therefore have a profound effect on a child's opportunity, relationship with his or her parents and siblings, and citizen status (Coe 2008). Younger children who are born in a country of migration that recognizes citizenship on the basis of place of birth are citizens, while parents and older children are not, or may even be present illegally and subject to deportation (Boehm 2011). Furthermore, older children "left behind" when a parent migrates can develop close relationships to grandparents, who may be called "mother" and "father," and to the other children a grandparent is raising: cousins who are taken as siblings (Rae-Espinoza 2011, Leinaweaver 2008). While separation from mothers and fathers is hard and has been well discussed in the literature on migration (Parreñas 2004; Suárez-Orozco, Todorova, and Louie 2002), so too can separation from siblings—a less well-studied area. Like educational policy, immigration regimes can heighten the differential experiences of siblings despite changing demographics that create more overlap between siblings.

Different state policies thus can have profound effects on siblingship as conceptualized and as lived. State policies are part of the social field in which people navigate the making, breaking, and renewal of relationships. Furthermore, state policies can generate significant changes in the social field quite quickly, with sibling relations serving as a buffer to mitigate these changes even as they are affected by them.

THE CHAPTERS

Although there are many cross-cutting issues among the collected papers, they are roughly grouped together in two clusters. One cluster focuses on ways siblingship is constructed as different ways of sharing (parentage, experience, or exchange) and transcends binary oppositions between descent and marriage, kinship and friendship (Pauli and Van der Geest). A second cluster explores the ways in which siblings affect individual life courses through time and in relation to different power positions (Alber, Obendiek, and Coe).

Julia Pauli's chapter, "'Sharing Made Us Sisters': Sisterhood, Migration, and Household Dynamics in Mexico and Namibia," deals with the largely neglected issue of relations between sisters, arguing that they are often central to the maintenance of households and families, particularly in the contexts of migration. In particular, she examines the conditions and experiences during childhood that foster close ties between sisters, using ethnographic information from long-term fieldwork in both Mexico and Namibia. Building on retrospective accounts of childhood, the influence of age and birth order on the experiences during childhood for two pairs of sisters is discussed. Migration, class formation, and transformations in household patterns have altered sisterly relations during their life courses, exhibiting how sisterhood is continuously formed and reformed.

Like Pauli, Sjaak van der Geest, in his chapter on "Kinship as Friendship: Brothers and Sisters in Kwahu, Ghana," examines the question of how meaningful sibling relations are constructed and maintained by looking at the paradoxical relationship between siblingship and friendship. They are in one respect each other's antipode, but they also share common sentiments of belonging and affection. This essay unravels the sometimes overlapping, sometimes opposing appearances of kinship and friendship, based on ethnographic observations and conversations in a rural Ghanaian community. In particular, Van der Geest argues that the friendship of the sibling is not simply given, handed down, and dictated by biology, tradition, or an older generation; it is a choice that people make in spite of kinship's constraints.

Although also concerned with the "making" of siblingship, the main focus of Erdmute Alber's chapter, "Within the Thicket of Intergenerational Sibling Relations: A Case Study from Northern Benin," shifts us to the second thematic cluster, exploring how siblings affect the life course of one another and others in different generations, in sometimes ambiguous ways. Alber centers her analysis on a family conflict in Northern Benin in which sibling relations played a key role. She argues that relations between siblings are critical to understanding fosterage arrangements and intergenerational relations. Second, the analysis stresses the ambivalences, power relations, and inequalities of sibling relations: on the one hand, it was the brothers and sisters of the girl's parents who brought her into the situation, but one the other hand, it was a brother who helped her to escape. Siblingship proves to be a key factor in understanding the pressures and forces of kinship relations as well as their potentiality in affecting a young person's life course.

Helena Obendiek, in her chapter "When Siblings Determine your 'Fate': Sibling Support and Educational Mobility in Rural Northwest China," is also interested in transformations in sibling relations in diachronic perspective, but here in relation to state policies. Focusing on how schooling mediates sibling relatedness, Obendiek demonstrates the ways in which changing conditions shape experiences of sibling relatedness and how, vice versa, sibling relatedness impacts educational opportunities (linked to social upward mobility) in rural China. During the first two decades of post-Maoist reform policies, educational achievement led to great socioeconomic differences within rural sibling sets. Graduates of this historical period often became the main supporters of their siblings in the countryside, usually giving their support indirectly and "diagonally" via the next generation. Since the late 1990s, reforms in the educational and labor sectors have tightened the interdependence of siblings' fates in poor rural regions of China, turning siblings not only into competitors for scarce family resources but also into important reserves of support. In conclusion, Obendiek—similar to Alber—is able to demonstrate the intergenerational effects of siblinghood and how changing policies altered opportunities as well as obligations related to siblinghood, thus deeply affecting local practices of sibling relatedness.

Finally, drawing on ethnographic observations and interviews, Cati Coe, in "Transnational Migration and Changes in Sibling Support in Ghana," examines the significance of siblingship for Ghanaian transnational migrants. Transnational migrants are relying on their siblings in familiar ways as a transnational strategy to foster their children. At the same time, fosterage is increasingly criticized discursively in Ghana, particularly within the social milieu from which transnational migrants tend to come. Therefore they are reviving a practice that their compatriots at home are increasingly regarding less favorably—as an option of last resort. This ongoing social change at home means that migrants feel ambivalence about using siblings as foster parents. Focusing on sibling relationships in the context of transnational migration highlights how people adapt kin relationships to new contexts and create new contexts out of existing expectations of kin. Like the chapters by Alber and Obendiek, Coe shows how siblings can be a source of support because of their different trajectories, as well as how sibling ties, through fostering, create relations across the generations.

CONCLUSION

In an article published in 1996, John Borneman argued that marriage still had a paradigmatic status in anthropology, despite all the critique. He urged that other forms of sexuality and (non)reproduction should be seen as equally important to kinship, and that marriage instability and exclusion should be viewed as counterparts of its inclusionary and stabilizing aspects. In this book, we make a similar argument in regards to siblingship as a relation formerly treated as "supplementary, if not insignificant, to marriage in particular, and to social structure in general" (Borneman 1996: 221). We can see this even in the work of Radcliffe-Brown, who pioneered the study of relations between siblings but still placed a married (male) ego at the center.

Despite Annette Weiner's earlier call (1992) for giving more attention to (cross-sex) sibling intimacy, our impression is that not much has changed. This has not even been done in kinship studies in Asian countries, where siblingship has been a more prominent topic in anthropological literature than in other regions like Africa, Europe, or Latin America. We argue that an emphasis on sibling relations would not only avoid reducing women's social roles to those of sexuality and human reproduction but also generate deeper insights into the nature of kinship in general.

Putting the various kinds of brotherly and sisterly relations at the center enhances the chances of understanding how relatedness is constructed precisely because of siblingship's fluid and flexible nature. Siblingship is sometimes conceived as rooted in common descent, as described by Radcliffe-Brown, or it might be a mythical starting point (with no procreation in advance) as is seemingly the case in Malaysia, as described by Carsten (1997). It is sometimes generated through growing up in one house and sharing childhoods, without implying shared (biological) parentage. And it is sometimes represented through mutual exchange and care. Taking this variety into account allows us to ask why and when these relations are installed with meaning, thereby becoming materially and emotionally significant. Thus we return to questions posed by classical kinship studies of what makes established relations worth maintaining or giving up and how that in turn contributes to community and identity processes and to material and emotional survival.

From our overview on the scattered reflections on siblingship in the anthropological literature, we draw a tentative systematization of the ways in which siblingship is conceived. There seem to be three broad patterns in how people imagine siblingship. One is on the basis of shared parentage; another is on the basis of shared childhoods and time spent together; a third is on the basis of reciprocal exchanges and care. These patterns lead to different perspectives. The focus on shared parentage—whether viewed as social or biological—highlights the significance of siblings for intergenerational relations, through their shared tie to the previous generation, and the possibility of constructing kin relationships in the next generation, and it seems to confirm more classical views of kinship. The second conceptualization raises questions about how similarity is constructed and sustained, particularly in childhood, on the basis of shared experience and positionality. The third conceptualization focuses attention on difference and the changing relations between siblings across the life course. The second and third perspectives confirm the emphasis of the new studies on the process and practices of making kinship. We argue that it is on the basis of its plurality of possibilities that siblingship, a largely neglected area in the anthropology of kinship, can contribute to our understanding of how humans create and maintain meaningful relations.

A perspective on sibling relations is especially suited to looking at constructing and maintaining relatedness across the life course. In addition, many social relations are constructed on an ideal relation of siblingship. This is true for kin and nonkin relations from the conjugal bond to larger communities, such as religious orders and nation-states. The collected essays, focused on the practices and notions of siblingship, contribute to a deeper understanding of how relatedness, closeness, and distance are negotiated across the life course and generations.

Acknowledgments

This book comes out of a workshop on "Brother- and Sister-hood" organized by Erdmute Alber and Sjaak van der Geest at the University of Bayreuth in November 2009. Thanks to the Bayreuth International Graduate School of African Studies (BIGSAS) for financing and logistic help. We are grateful to Julia Pauli, Sjaak van der Geest, and an anonymous reviewer for their comments on the introduction.

PART 1

SIBLINGSHIP AS SHARED PARENTAGE AND EXPERIENCE

CHAPTER 2

"SHARING MADE US SISTERS"
SISTERHOOD, MIGRATION, AND HOUSEHOLD
DYNAMICS IN MEXICO AND NAMIBIA

Julia Pauli

It almost felt like an ethnographic déjà vu. I was chatting with Mona, a teacher in her forties, in front of her house in Fransfontein, northwest Namibia, when Christina joined us.[1] Mona and same-aged Christina had grown up together. They considered and called each other sisters—*!gasas* in the local language Khoekhoegowab. Mona was telling me about her recent health problems, especially high blood pressure and shortness of breath, and the little help she received from those around her in her household. But then Mona smiled, looking at Christina, and proclaimed that Christina was the only one who was really there for her, who cared for her. I asked the two why this is so, and they replied, "Because we are sisters. We are similar. Growing up together made us sisters."

Seven years earlier, in November 1996 and in a very different setting—the community Pueblo Nuevo in the central highlands of Mexico—Ana and Alicia, then in their late twenties, had told me almost the same thing about their relationship as sisters. Ana had just suffered from a nervous breakdown after a severe fight with a neighbor, and Alicia was taking care of her. When I asked her why she was helping Ana so much, she looked at me with surprise. Then Alicia emphasized that because she and Ana had suffered and grown up together, they would always be there for each other: "Sharing made us sisters." Thus both the Mexican and the Namibian sisters emphasize

that growing up together is a central way of sharing and becoming
related as sisters.

During my fieldwork in Mexico and Namibia, I rarely encountered
other types of social relations characterized by the casual intensity of
adult sisters. I call it "casual" because, in general, sisters did not make
a big fuss about these social backbones of their lives. This unpreten-
tious attitude differed strongly from the public performances and
ritualized nature of other kin relations, such as *compadrazgo* relations
with nonrelatives in Mexico (Schnegg 2005, 2007) or splendid marriage celebrations in Namibia (Pauli n.d.). Yet it was intense, because
many women in both settings, albeit acknowledging conflict and
rivalry between sisters, stressed the centrality of at least one sister in
their lives and maintained strong bonds to a sister.

The stability and long-term endurance of these sisterly bonds is also
remarkable because both communities are characterized by translocal
livelihoods, exhibiting high levels of migration and dynamic household
structures. The Mexican community has a long history of national and
transnational migration, mainly to US destinations. There is no one
in the village whose life has not been significantly shaped by migration, and almost all adults have migration experiences themselves.
Although the Namibian community has a very different history, life
trajectories are as much intertwined with migration processes and
resulting household dynamics as in the Mexican case. Colonialism
and Apartheid forced people into specific territories and migration
patterns. Migration became the central way for most households and
individuals to adapt and survive. Today, translocal migration within
Namibia continues to be of central importance, and only a few individuals are able to permanently live in Fransfontein.

Thus, in both settings, individuals have to create and maintain
close sisterly ties against a background of ever-changing and spatially
extended family networks and households. As research on transnational
family life has aptly shown, translocal livelihoods offer opportunities
to reconfigure family roles and relations, and pose the challenge to
constantly adapt to new social situations (Bryceson and Vuorela 2002,
Erel 2002, Pauli 2008). What explains the importance of sisterly ties
in these highly mobile and dynamic settings?

My approach to answer this question will be twofold. On the one
hand, I want to understand how, why, and between whom sisterly

bonds are formed in childhood in the two research settings. On the other hand, I want to explore how these relations are being maintained over time against the background of high levels of migration and dynamic household structures in both Namibia and Mexico. My central thesis is that through the sharing of emotionally charged experiences during childhood, some siblings are drawn together in a closeness that often remains life long despite ruptures thereafter.

The importance of sharing substances and practices to become and remain related has already been highlighted in kinship studies (Alber, Beer, Pauli, and Schnegg 2010; Böck and Rao 2000; Carsten 2000, 2004; Marshall 1977; Pauli 2006). Further, in her autobiography, *Blackberry Winter*, Margaret Mead, who grew up with three sisters and one brother, notes, "In addition to their shared memories of childhood and of their relationships to each other's children, they share memories of the same home, the same homemaking style…But above all, perhaps, sisters who have grown up close to one another know how their daydreams have been interwoven with their life experiences" (Mead 1972: 70). Mead's observation stresses the importance of shared memories of childhood and awareness of one another's dreams for the maintenance of sibling ties in adult life. Unlike a woman's parents, who normally die at a certain point of her life course; her spouse, who often steps into her life after childhood and adolescence; and her children, who in general will survive her, sisters (and brothers) have the potential to be present during most of her life. Thus, as Mead writes, given this long-term perspective, sisters know especially well about the ruptures and fulfillments of the others' desires and life plans. Sister-sister relations have thus a particularly strong potential to result in intimate but also competitive relationships. Further, the potentially life-long quality of this relationship fosters evaluations of the sisterly tie at different moments in the life course and against the background of one's own accomplishments and failures. However, whether adult sisters stress differences or similarities in their achievements and failures may vary, as the comparison of my two sisterly tales will show. Competing sisters may overemphasize differences, while hierarchical stability between sisters may foster discourses of equality.

Margaret Mead's observations also point to the fact that anthropological research on sisterhood needs a life-course perspective and has to go beyond focusing on socialization processes only, as much previous research has done (Ervin-Tripp 1989, Lancy 2008, Weisner and Gallimore 1977, Zukow 1989). In adulthood, sister relations seem to almost disappear from the anthropological record. Moreover, as Jennifer Johnson-Hanks (2002) has shown, life history research also tends to focus on the transformations from one life stage to the next, not realizing enough that a new "stage" can include previous identities and roles (see also Alber, in this volume). The lack of research about adult sisterhood might also result from anthropology's stronger concentration on systems than on individuals and their specific histories. The main axiom of the two classic anthropological kinship theories, alliance theory and descent theory, is the transformation of sisters into wives and mothers. That women nevertheless remain sisters, while becoming wives and mothers, is overlooked.

Research on matrifocality and matrifocal household patterns also focuses on women as mothers and constructs the kinship universe around relations of descent—that is, between mothers and daughters. But matrifocal households may be better perceived as networks of women (Blackwood 2005, Cornwall 2005) very often including ties between sisters. Linked to the high levels of migration, matrifocal households are widespread in the Namibian and the Mexican communities analyzed here. For a substantial number of these Namibian and Mexican households, sisterly ties are even more important than mother-daughter links. An extension of the concept of matrifocality is thus needed to better understand the household patterns described here. I propose the term *femifocality* to highlight the centrality of women within these household networks and to overcome the matrifocal bias of perceiving central women in these households as only mothers or daughters. The term *sorofocality* could also be used. However, I decided against this term because it is as limiting as *matrifocality*. As my two ethnographic cases will show, femifocal households can sometimes be more matrifocal and at other times more sorofocal, depending on the specific needs of individuals and the compositions of households at different moments in time.[2]

Based on their narrations and my own observations, I will describe the two sister relationships—that is, Mona and Christina from Namibia and Ana and Alicia from Mexico—from childhood until adulthood.[3] To further frame my empirical findings, in the next section I will provide some background information on the two case studies. Special attention will be given to household and migration patterns.

TRANSLOCAL LIVELIHOODS AND DYNAMIC HOUSEHOLD PATTERNS IN MEXICO AND NAMIBIA

I met the Mexican sisters Ana and Alicia for the first time in June 1996 when I started my fieldwork in the rural community of Pueblo Nuevo in central Mexico.[4] From June 1996 until July 1997, one of the sisters, Ana, worked as my field assistant. Additionally, my husband and fellow anthropologist Michael Schnegg and I became *compadres* ("coparents") of both sisters and their husbands in 1997. In 2000, 2001, and 2010, we revisited the village and stayed with Ana's family.

Pueblo Nuevo is located in the valley of Solís and is part of the Estado de México in the central highlands of Mexico. As in other parts of Mexico, within the last eighty years, national and international migration has played an important role in transforming the economic foundation of the village from subsistence-oriented land cultivation into transnational and diversified networks. National migration, mainly to Mexico City, started during the 1960s. Locally, international migration, in particular to the United States, dates back to the 1980s during a severe breakdown of the Mexican economy. While both men and women from Pueblo Nuevo migrate within Mexico, female migration to the United States remains rare. During our last visit in 2010, only a few men, mainly elderly or disabled villagers, had not migrated to the United States at least once. In many cases, international migration is practiced by young and middle-aged men who want to accumulate enough money to build a house or invest in a small business.

Thus house building has become a major activity in the village (Pauli 2008). In 2010, we observed a fascinating variety of forms, styles, and house materials, ranging from so-called local houses made out of *adobe* and *teja*, a roofing tile produced in the village, to futuristic glass constructions with panoramic views or colorful cement palaces painted in mint green or raspberry rose. Many of the fancy and expensive houses were occupied by wives and children of absent husbands living on the other side of the border in Chicago, Los Angeles, or "*las Carolinas*"—North and South Carolina. This household pattern strongly diverges from what David Robichaux in his comparative analysis has called "the Mesoamerican household formation system" (1997: 15), characterized by virilocal residence and ultimogeniture. Although the majority of households in Pueblo Nuevo followed this pattern until the mid-1990s, today household patterns are much more fluid and dynamic. Instead of living (and very often suffering) with their mother-in-laws, women prefer to either stay on their own in their newly built houses or temporarily move in with their own natal kin, especially sisters and mothers, while their husbands migrate. The temporary absence of husbands thus stimulated reconfigurations of gender, kin, and generational relations, especially a strengthening of what I call femifocal household structures and kin ties to mothers and sisters (Pauli 2008). A similar importance of femifocality can be observed in the Namibian households.

Information on the Namibian case is based on joint fieldwork with Michael Schnegg in the Fransfontein area from May 2003 until October 2004 and the summers of 2005 and 2006.[5] Michael and I first met the two Namibian sisters Mona and Christina in the summer of 2003. From 2003 until 2004, Christina helped us with the care for our young daughter. Although Namibia's Apartheid policy was based on the idea of "separate development" and a division into ethnically homogeneous "homelands," in reality the homelands neither were ethnically homogeneous nor were many people able to live in them. Consequently, migration between rural and urban areas was very common (Barnard 1992: 213, Jauch 1998: 28, Rohde 1997: 259). In this region of Namibia, both men and women have migrated. With Namibian independence in 1990, the situation has not changed significantly, and many people continue to migrate back and forth between rural Fransfontein and different urban areas, especially Windhoek and Walvis Bay (Greiner 2011).

Only the wealthy and the old do not migrate. Approximately 16 percent of the Fransfontein households can be classified as wealthy, including better-paid government employees like teachers working for the local primary school, so-called traditional authorities, local administrators, and a few wealthy livestock owners (Pauli n.d.).[6] All other households are characterized by a steady flux of people. This is especially true for the female-headed households representing 49 percent of Fransfontein households. Heads of these households are mostly elderly women receiving the pensions to which all Namibian citizens sixty years and older are entitled. In some cases, the female head is younger and employed in one of the government institutions. Daughters, granddaughters, sisters, sons, lovers, and other kin cluster around the female heads. However, if household income becomes strained or there is a chance to get work somewhere else, household members readily leave. Femifocality is further fostered by a phenomenon Jane Guyer has labeled "polyandrous motherhood" (Guyer 1994)—that is, unmarried women who consecutively have children with two, three, or more different partners. Within these household structures, child fosterage (locally called *groot maak kinders*, Afrikaans for "children one raises") is very common. Contrary to Erdmute Alber's findings on the strong normative pressure to participate in child fosterage in Benin (see Alber, this volume), Fransfontein child fosterage is mainly practiced for pragmatic reasons. Nevertheless, in some cases, a grandmother or a sister has asked for a child to stay with her. Although there are exceptions, most women prefer to leave their children in the care of their natal kin and not the kin group of the child's father. Further, marriage rates have dramatically declined during the last few decades, and the involvement of unmarried fathers with their out-of-wedlock children is limited overall (Pauli 2012). Maternal grandmothers with stable pensions or employed sisters with reliable wages are especially preferred caregivers. Mona and Christina's sisterhood, described in the next section, will provide further details on these practices.

Thus, despite very different histories and political economies, both settings exhibit similarities regarding the effects migration had on household patterns. Femifocal households are widespread and present in both settings. However, femifocality is often only temporary in Mexico, while femifocal household structures are much more permanent in Namibia. Nevertheless, in both cases the emergence and/ or persistence of femifocal household patterns stimulated through migration has opened up and extended female social spaces. This has also fostered ties between sisters, as the following in-depth analysis of the two sister pairs underscores.

Although chronologically the Mexican case would be first, only with my Namibian research did I start to reflect and analyze the importance of shared experiences for the formation and maintenance of sibling ties. *Kai//are*, the Khoekhoegowab expression for being related through growing up together and sharing essential childhood experiences, inspired me to inquire how important growing up together is for kin ties in other cultural contexts.[7] After discussing the relation between the two Namibian sisters, Christina and Mona, for specific periods of time during their lives and as embedded in their wider kin network, I will then analyze the relation between the Mexican sisters, Ana and Alicia. In the final part, I will summarize similarities and differences between the two cases and discuss how far varying structural conditions like the wider political economic context, migration patterns, and specific family and household structures influence how the two pairs of sisters have practiced and lived out their relationship over time.

The Namibian Sisters Christina and Mona: "Growing Up Together Made Us Sisters"

The first time I saw the sisters Christina and Mona during a school event at the local Fransfontein primary school in July 2003, I was astonished by how different they looked. While Christina was tall and thin and always on the move running after children, Mona was full-figured and self-contained, remaining seated throughout the event. Mona's gracious calm was also a reflection of her class position. As a teacher, she belonged to the local elite, while Christina, a temporary domestic worker, was part of the crowd. How close the two women actually were became evident a couple of weeks later when we searched for someone to take care of our daughter Liliana and Mona recommended Christina to us. Mona stressed that because she had grown up with Christina, she knew her especially well. Further, she wanted to help her sister, who at that time, due to severe health problems, desperately needed some cash income.

In the course of the following year, we got to know both women and their families quite well. We learned that from a genealogical point of view, Christina was not Mona's sister but her aunt or "small mother"—in Khoekhoegowab *maros* (mother's younger sister). Nevertheless, they called each other sisters, *!gasas*, and stressed that this is the best term to describe their relationship. This kind of extension of the sibling category is very much in line with a rather flexible use of kin terms in Fransfontein in general. In the Damara and Nama[8] kinship terminology (which dominates local discourse), male and female parallel cousins (mother's sister's or father's brother's children) are also classified as brothers and sisters. They are addressed in the same way as siblings or half-siblings: for younger brothers, *!gasab*; for older brothers, *abutib*; for younger sisters, *!guisas*; and for older sisters: *ausis*. In everyday practice, the naming might be simplified. The kin term *!gasab/s* (*b* = male and *s* = female singular ending) may be applied to indicate a sibling relation. On the other hand, cross cousins (mother's brother's or father's sister's children) have their own kin terms: */gamareb* and */aisas*. Here, no age differentiation is used. Unlike the sibling relations, relations with */gamareb* and */aisas* are often joking relations and might have sexual connotations. People comment that marriage between cross cousins used to be preferential. Today, this type of marriage is extremely rare. Contrary to the cross-cousin relation and in line with the classification of parallel cousins as siblings, sexual relations with parallel cousins are perceived as incestuous.

Why then did the two women insist that they are sisters and not aunt / small mother (mother's younger sister) and niece/daughter (sister's daughter)?[9] When we asked them this question, they stressed that "growing up together made us sisters." An episode we witnessed in April 2004 sheds further light on the local meanings of *kai//are*, or growing up together.

After an absence of more than two days, we observed the return of several preschool children to the Fransfontein village. The children had walked to and from one of the distant communal settlements in the very sparsely populated Fransfontein area. Upon their return, they were (at least in my perception) rather casually and without any further comment welcomed by their families. I was absolutely astonished by the event. Maybe the presence of our then two-year-old daughter intensified my feelings and inspired me even more to reflect on the observation. Michael and I started to ask adults and children if it was common that children were "left alone" for such long periods of time. Indeed, it was. Yet the idea that the children are "left alone" was wrong.[10] Repeatedly, we were told that children are never alone—because there are always sisters and brothers around them, taking care. This, of course, matches research on the relevance of children and siblings as care givers (Weisner and Gallimore 1977, Zukow 1989). In Fransfontein, care is not only given from older to younger siblings. Due to the general low level of parental involvement, similar-aged siblings also maintain strong caring relations. Yet most of the research on siblinghood and caring does not ask what the long-term social effects of these socialization and caring practices might be; the focus is on the socialization period and not on other phases of the life cycle. However, many Fransfonteiners were very explicit in highlighting to us that growing up together, *kai//are*, and living together through extreme and key experiences formed the most intense, trusting, caring, and long-lasting relations in their lives. To better understand why growing up together is of such significance for sibling ties, a focus on the circumstances under which the two Namibian sisters Christina and Mona have grown up together will provide some further insights.

Christina was born in 1962 as the last daughter of Martha. A year later, in 1963, Martha's second daughter Rebeca gave birth to Mona. After weaning little Mona, Rebeca decided that the baby girl should grow up with her mother Martha, Mona's grandmother, on her communal farm in Rehoboth, south of the country's capital Windhoek. Thus Mona and Christina grew up together at the Rehoboth farm, only a year apart in age. Rebeca, Mona's mother, was working as a domestic servant in Windhoek, providing the extended family in Windhoek and Rehoboth with food and clothing. In her narrative, Mona highlights the similarities between her mother at that time and herself as a mother and caretaker today: "My mother was working in Windhoek. She always went down to Rehoboth to the farm after getting paid to give us food. My mother was like me, similar to what I am doing now. She was doing that job, looking after the family, always looking after the family" (Interview with Mona, September 2004).

Until age nine, Mona stayed with her grandmother Martha. Then Mona moved to Windhoek and started schooling. Four years later and already a teenager, Christina followed Mona to Windhoek and also started schooling. Christina says that she started school so late because her mother did not want to let her go, as she was her youngest daughter. In Windhoek, Christina and Mona stayed together again, living in the house of Mona's mother Rebeca in Katutura, Windhoek's township.

The circumstances under which Mona and Christina grew up together are exemplary of the childhood experiences of many Fransfontein people and further illuminate the more general pattern of the entanglements between migration and femifocal households. Mona and Christina's multilocal household is connected through a number of femifocal links. Further, femifocality fostered through "polyandrous motherhood" (Guyer 1994) is also very present in Mona and Christina's multilocal household. The four women mentioned previously all have children with more than one partner: Martha has children with two, Rebeca with four, Christina with three, and Mona with two different partners. Some of these children stay with their mothers, but most of them live at least temporarily and often for many years (like Mona) in the care of other female relatives. Their mothers are not "careless" but caring differently, as Mona described.[11] Exchange of services like child care for cash and goods purchased in the city are vital for the survival of both the urban and the rural branches of a household, as the transactions between Mona's grandmother Martha and Mona's mother Rebeca exemplify. Due to this specific household and family situation, which itself is the result of the complex entanglements of migration and the broader political and economic situation, Christina and Mona have spent most of their childhood together. Thus "growing up together made them sisters," as they repeatedly stressed in our conversations.

I now want to turn to the kind of shared experiences that have shaped these intense feelings of closeness and relatedness during socialization and in later life. During a joint interview with both women, Mona described their shared childhood experiences as follows: "We ate together, we slept together, she helped me when I was beaten, I helped her when she was beaten. She feels the same pains as I do; she washes me when I am sick, she makes food for me when I am sick" (Interview with Mona and Christina, August 2006). As Mona's descriptions show, the key experiences[12] children live through while growing up together are very physical and often center on bodily needs and pains, especially hunger, thirst, shelter, and corporal punishment. Food, often only maize flour, is served to children in one bowl, and all children eat together.

Further, children share beds or sleeping places. Corporal punishment of children is common. If children are beaten, they do not search for relief from their parents or other caretakers but from other children, the ones they grow up with. Mona emphasizes that Christina is the most important person in her life. She thinks that she knows her better than anybody else. Mona also stresses that she likes Christina to be in her house because it reminds her of the time they shared a

Figure 2.1   Children Sharing Food (Namibia, 2006)

sleeping mat. It calms Mona to know that her sister is there. Through numerous moments of shared closeness and care, within a given context of household and kinship relations, sisterhood (and brotherhood) is formed. Such moments shape whom, out of an often rather large pool of possible brothers and sisters, one feels close to.[13] Not growing up together, on the other hand, means not sharing key experiences. And not sharing these central and formative moments during childhood often implies feeling either not or only slightly related.

There are two peculiarities of Christina and Mona's sisterhood. For one, Christina and Mona are very close in age. Second, they have grown up together in a very remote environment with specific concepts of parent- and childhood. I will discuss these items in turn.

It is an open question about whether a greater age difference might have changed the relation between Christina and Mona. Many women stressed that relations with those sisters (and brothers) "next to oneself," sisters (or brothers) born directly before or after one and thus usually close in age, are also emotionally close. The relations with siblings more distant in the birth order and thus in age was often very different, sometimes even aloof.[14] Older and younger sisters experience situations together, but they perceive the situations from different perspectives. Similarly aged sisters are in a better position to mutually understand one another's feelings. Thus I want to argue that *kai//are* (growing up together) sisterhood is closely linked to *similarly responding to and remembering* key experiences—not only experiencing them together.

Another peculiarity of Christina and Mona's sisterhood is the social and ecological environment in which they grew up. As mentioned before, in the rural setting discussed here, even very young children are left in the care of other children most of the time. There is almost no motor vehicle traffic in the area, and children learn early on to detect and handle situations involving dangerous animals, especially snakes and scorpions. The situation in Windhoek and other urban areas is quite different, and thus risks for children and concepts of child- and parenthood might vary significantly.

The *kai//are* sisterhood between Christina and Mona affects their relations today. Relations resulting from *kai//are* are very often long-term, in many cases life-long, relations. Yet, like all other social relations, *kai//are* relations are never static but are continuously remade under changing conditions. A central moment of transformation occurred when Mona continued schooling and eventually became a teacher, while Christina dropped out of school after only a few years and started working as a domestic servant. Today, class differences between the two women are very pronounced. While Mona's privileged position as a teacher allows her a high level of autonomous decision making and life planning, Christina depends very much on others and especially on Mona to go on with her life. When we met the two women in 2003, they were living together in Mona's house. The relationship resembled a husband-housewife relationship with Mona as the breadwinner and Christina as the housewife. Several months later, in 2004, Mona decided to send Christina to take care of her house in Windhoek. Mona had inherited the house from her mother. Christina did not like the idea of being alone in Windhoek, separated from her children who would remain in Fransfontein. Christina wanted to stay in Mona's house in Fransfontein but was not able to prevail against Mona's request. Drawing on their close relation, Mona argued that Christina was the only one she could trust enough to take good care of her property. Previously, Mona had been disappointed by a not-so-close female cousin who had mistreated her Windhoek house and had not followed Mona's housekeeping rules. Thus, although Christina was economically dependent on Mona, Mona also depended on Christina. On several occasions, Mona underscored that Christina is one of the very few people she really trusts. This deep level of trust resulting from the shared experiences and memories of key moments during childhood may help to explain why, despite fundamental economic differences between the sisters, Christina and Mona always stressed their equality to one another in our conversations. Contrary to this sisterly discourse highlighting similarity despite differences, the Mexican sisters Ana and Alicia are much more ambivalent regarding their relationship with each other.

Like the Namibian sisters, Ana and Alicia also shared key experiences from growing up together. In both cases, the sharing of central experiences from a similar vantage point is decisive for the formation and maintenance of these sisterly ties in adulthood. However, although sharing key experiences during childhood may create a close bond, it does not necessarily prevent jealousy and competition in adulthood, as the case study of the Mexican sisters Ana and Alicia will show. Although economically more similar to each other than the Namibian sisters, they do not always perceive and stress this similarity. Similarity and difference, and care and competition alternate in their relationship. After describing the relationship between Ana and Alicia, I explore why these differences in adult sisterhood emerge, despite shared experiences in childhood.

THE MEXICAN SISTERS ANA AND ALICIA: BETWEEN CARE AND COMPETITION

Similar to the Namibian narrative, movement and migration figure prominently in the Mexican case. As a teenager, Roberta, Ana and Alicia's mother, worked as a domestic servant in Mexico City, where she met Ana and Alicia's father, who was working as a driver. They fell in love and he took her with him to his home community Pueblo Nuevo, about a four-hour drive from Mexico City by bus. There, the young couple got married. Then Pedro and Roberta moved back to Mexico City. Roberta and Pedro's first child, Ana, was born in 1969 in Mexico City. With her infant, Roberta moved back to Pueblo Nuevo while

Pedro continued to work in Mexico City. In 1972, Alicia was born. In 1973, Pedro Junior, the family's only son, followed. Roberta gave birth to three more daughters: Roberta Junior in 1977, Lola in 1983, and Anabella in 1988.

Ana and Alicia both grew up in Pueblo Nuevo and did not leave the village until they reached adolescence. Most of the time, both parents stayed with them and their other siblings.[15] There are two main themes in the narratives of the two sisters of their childhood and teenage years: on the one hand, they stressed how demanding it was for them to be the two eldest sisters and to take care of their younger siblings. On the other hand, they highlighted that these circumstances drew them closer together. Contrary to their other siblings, they experienced things together and in a similar way. The preferential treatment of two of their siblings, their only brother Pedro and their youngest sister Anabella, was especially a nuisance for the two sisters, as Ana explained to me:

> Oh, our sister Anabella, every day she got money to spend at school! And she could also go to the shop at school, and every week our father would pay her out. For Alicia and me, he did not do anything like that. And my brother was also different; you know, he was the only son. When he was born my father was so happy. And you know, my brother liked to get rid of his shoes and his trousers, running around without them. When my father saw that he beat Alicia and me and said we should take care of our brother. And we told our brother, "Please, please don't do that." But he, he did not care. They just preferred him over us. And you know, my brother and my younger sisters, they did not suffer like us, like Alicia and I suffered. (Interview with Ana, March 1997)[16]

As Ana and Alicia's narrative shows, it was not only the birth order and age of the siblings that lead to these vastly different experiences of childhood but also gender. According to Ana and Alicia, their brother was in a much more privileged position during his childhood. In several of my life history interviews with women who were also older sisters, comparable complaints to the ones of Ana and Alicia were articulated. For example, Giselda, Ana's neighbor, born in 1961 as a first child, told me that she did not have any childhood at all (see Pauli 2000: 186–87): "Well, I hardly had any childhood because I always had to take care of my brother and sisters. And I helped my mother. When I was allowed to play once in a while, I had to take my younger brother with me. I did not have any childhood. When I came home from school I had to help my mother with the younger children. I never did anything alone" (Interview with Giselda, April 1997). While many older or eldest sisters in Namibia and Mexico felt overly burdened by their responsibilities, some nevertheless stressed that this also fostered an especially intense tie to the sister closest in age to them. On many occasions, Ana and Alicia remarked that looking at the life of their sister was like looking in a mirror, reflecting back their own situation. This gave them great comfort in difficult situations, such as domestic violence or first menstruation.[17] However, as will be shown next, in adulthood it also led to evaluations of their own life in comparison to their sister's, generating rivalry. Unlike younger siblings who were treated differently by the parents and were generally perceived as, in Alicia's words, "living in a different time," Ana and Alicia expected to see and feel the same way.

Beyond childhood, the life histories of the sisters continued to exhibit a high degree of similarity. Both went to Mexico City as teenagers. At age eighteen, Ana got pregnant. Six months into the pregnancy, her boyfriend died. Ana returned to her parent's house and in 1988 gave birth to a daughter. When her daughter turned a year old, she left her in the care of her mother Roberta in Pueblo Nuevo and moved again to Mexico City. Around the same time, Alicia started working in a factory in Mexico City. The sisters stressed how close they were during that time, always helping each other, caring for one another, and spending their leisure time together.

Their paths began to diverge with their marriages. Ana met her husband Leo and moved in with Leo's parents, while Alicia continued working in Mexico City. However, at Ana and Leo's wedding, Alicia fell in love with Leo's younger brother Raimundo and also moved in with Leo and Raimundo's parents. In 1993, Ana gave birth to her second child, a son. In 1994, Alicia gave birth to her first child, Esperanza. By that time, and after a severe period of conflict with her mother-in-law, Ana had persuaded her father to give her a piece of land adjacent to his house. Leo built a small house, and Ana and Leo moved next to Ana's parents. Alicia remained in her mother-in-law's house, suffering and sad.

This was basically the situation when I met the sisters for the very first time in 1996. While Ana was outgoing, talkative, and self-confident, residing rather contently in a house of her own next to her parents, Alicia, living in her mother-in-law's house, appeared shy, frustrated, and even sad (see Pauli 2008: 171). Ana's husband Leo, a man with many talents and contacts in the Mexican countryside, was busy working in a neighboring village, while Alicia's husband Raimundo had been unemployed for a long time. Ana was very much aware of these differences between herself and her sister closest in age. She tried to comfort and support Alicia as much as she could. Indicating their closeness, for the baptism of their only son Ana and her husband Leo decided to choose Alicia and Raimundo as the godparents. Within the *compadrazgo* system, even more important than the creation of a relation between the *padrinos* ("godparents") and the *ahijado* ("godchild") is the relation created between the two sets of parents (Schnegg 2005, Schnegg 2006). The child's parents and the godparents become *compadres* ("coparents"). In Pueblo Nuevo, it is very common to choose close siblings as godparents for one's children. This practice publically expresses and reinforces close sibling ties. Everyone knows which sibling has been chosen. In public, they will call each other *compadres*, thus stressing the extension of their kinship tie (for a comparable overlayering of kin and social roles, see Obendiek, this volume). Similarly, Ana and Alicia do not call each other sisters (*hermanas*) but use *comadre* ("comother") as their term of address.

Until the end of my fieldwork in July 1997, the living circumstances between the two sisters remained unequal. Ana was content, living in her own house and getting along well with her husband, while her sister Alicia was unhappy with most aspects of her life, including the lethargy of her husband and the meanness of her mother-in-law.

On my return in 2000, I was greatly surprised by fundamental changes both in the appearance of the two sisters and in their relation to each other. In 1998, like many other men from the valley, Alicia's husband Raimundo had migrated to the United States without authorization. With the incoming remittances, Alicia built a two-story house and filled it with consumer goods. When I saw Alicia again in 2000, she could hardly hide her triumph, showing me in great detail everything she had accomplished in her own house. Ana was jealous of her sister's success and house building and frustrated that in early 2000 her husband Leo had been caught at the US-Mexico border and deported back to Mexico. Over the next few years, the relation between the two sisters was tense.

This changed again around 2003. Despite having been deported in 2000 from the United States, in 2003 Leo managed to receive legal contracts with US employers. With his remittances, they enlarged their house, invested in animals, and bought consumer goods. Most important, however, they financed their daughter's teacher training at a private college. Around 2005, the relationship between the two sisters Ana and Alicia was rather calm and supportive once again. Both enjoyed enlarging and beautifying their houses. Further, because of the absences of their husbands, the sisters once again spent a lot of time together. Temporarily, they formed a femifocal household when Alicia moved in with Ana. Alicia wanted to spend as much time with Ana as possible and thought it was a waste of time to travel back and forth between the houses. Further, she commented to me that with Raimundo being "*al otro lado*" ("on the other side")—that is, in the United States—no one would care how well her house was kept. Instead, she could enjoy afternoons and evenings together with her sister, watching their favorite *telenovelas*.

Then, on my recent return in 2010, I was able to witness yet another twist in the relationship between the two sisters. With the economic crisis, Alicia's husband (and with him many other men from the valley) decided that it was too costly and risky to continue to cross the border illegally. Many men have remained in Mexico since. It was again Alicia's turn to be frustrated. Leo and Ana, however, started to reap the fruits of their investment in their daughter's education. The daughter had just started working as a teacher, substantially supporting her parents. Alicia was jealous of the success of her sister's daughter. To add to her troubles, Alicia's own daughter was struggling in school. At that moment in time, the sisters' relationship consisted mainly of competition and jealousy, contrary to the many moments of care and support that I had witnessed in earlier years.

Unlike the two Namibian sisters Mona and Christina, who despite their economic differences, characterized their relation as supportive and egalitarian in all their interactions with me, Ana and Alicia at times stressed their similarities but at other times underscored how different they were. For example, when Alicia had just finished building her house, Ana told me that she would never show off as much as her sister did: "Now that she has money, Alicia thinks she is better than me. I don't like that. I would not do that" (Interview with Ana, September 2000). Nevertheless, despite the ups and downs of their relationship, Ana and Alicia, like Mona and Christina, viewed their sisterly tie as one of the most important in their lives, firmly based on the joint memories of their shared experiences while growing up together. In adult life, sisterhood was constantly renewed and remade by dynamic household compositions, including periods of femifocality enabled by repeated migration experiences.

Conclusion

As my comparison of the two sister tales shows, despite substantial differences in conditions and contexts, in several important aspects the two cases exhibit similarities. Both narratives clearly demonstrate the relevance of sharing emotionally charged experiences during childhood for the formation of strong sisterly ties. What kind of experiences these may be varies by context.

The two settings can be classified as rural. Nevertheless, in Pueblo Nuevo, adult control of children's behavior is stricter than in Namibia, where children are often left by themselves. Consequently, the Namibian sisters Mona and Christina highlight how they managed their childhood basically on their own, sharing a sleeping mat, food, and sickness, while the Mexican sisters Ana and Alicia describe how their joint frustration over being responsible, and punished, for the misbehavior of their younger siblings drew them close together. Yet both tales also indicate that the relatedness (or kinship) that is formed out of these lived experiences is also structured by similar vantage points from which the pairs of sisters perceive events. Their similarity in age and gender and closeness in birth order thus frames their lived realities and draws them closer together. These "givens"—age, birth order, and gender—do not determine the sister relations, though, as becomes evident when one widens the focus and traces the sisters' relations beyond childhood.

Unlike other kin relations that will dissolve through death (parents) or appear only later in life (children), from an individual's perspective, sibling relations are extremely long lasting and often life long. This potentially life-long quality also fosters evaluations of the sisterly tie at different moments in the life course and against the background of one's own accomplishments and failures. Margaret Mead has captured this dimension of sisterly ties fittingly in her observation that "sisters who have grown up close to one another know how their daydreams have been interwoven with their life experiences" (Mead 1972: 70). The Mexican sisters Ana and Alicia stress how they are mirrors to each other. Yet a gaze into this sisterly mirror does not reveal a simple double of oneself but is also an evaluation of one's own situation. Further, only through a focus on the lived biographies of the two pairs of sisters through time has it become possible to reveal the ambivalence such a long-term relation also implies. The knowledge the sisters have gathered about the fortunes and failures of the other creates both deep feelings of similarity and strong emotions of jealousy and competition. In adult life, both pairs of sisters have to deal with their economic and status differences.

While the Mexican sisters sometimes openly compete with each other, the Namibian sisters have a more hierarchical and uncontested relationship. In the Mexican case, economic differences are temporary in nature and are examples of class dynamics and differentiations stimulated through transnational migration within an emerging middle class and consumer culture. These differences (and also similarities) are perceived and articulated by the Mexican sisters. In the Namibian case, there exists a strong and stable economic hierarchy between the two sisters. With her employment as a teacher in the 1990s, Mona joined the small local economic elite. Throughout her life, Christina never had secure employment. She always depended on others, especially her sister Mona, for survival. Nevertheless, Christina and Mona, despite pronounced and rather stable economic differences, highlighted how similar and equal they are through growing up together—kai//are. That Ana and Alicia's reflections on their relationship are more in accordance with the lived dynamics of the relationship is probably a result of their overall greater similarity, in economic and social terms, compared to the Namibian sisters. They do not economically depend on each other, and it is easier for them to criticize each other. This may explain why the articulation of competition is a central facet of sisterhood in the Mexican but not the Namibian narratives. Nevertheless, despite the ambivalence embedded in the sister relations, sharing (during childhood) made them sisters, and the joint memories stemming from that time, alongside later mutual experiences, keep them sisters through conflict and difference.

Both cases also underscore that sisterhood has to be seen as part of a multiplicity of kin roles embedded into a woman's life course (see also Alber, this volume). The Mexican case in particular exhibits the complex entanglements of two kin roles: sister and wife. The practice of Ana and Alicia's sisterhood strongly varies with the changing economic conditions and household patterns, especially their husbands' economic and migratory successes, leading to both competition and care between the sisters. Further, the absence of the migrating husbands and the emergence of temporary femifocal household patterns have also created new social spaces to live out sisterhood. Because of changing household patterns due to migration, intense sisterly ties during adulthood have become possible and at the same time necessary to endure and also enjoy everyday life. Similar to other transnational communities, these social practices and changing household patterns reconfigure kin, gender, and generational relations.

Similarly, the widespread practice of femifocal and multilocal households in the Fransfontein case also fosters close bonds between the adult sisters Mona and Christina. In the Namibian case it is not the recent absence of a migrating husband and an avoidance of a life in the mother-in-law's house that strengthens sisterly ties and leads to femifocality. For decades, multilocal households in Damaraland have used femifocal ties to facilitate their survival. Fransfontein households centered on related women—mothers, daughters, and sisters—arguably both have the necessary closeness to endure and are at the same flexible enough, such as through the migration of some household members, to accommodate to very difficult life circumstances. Hence, despite marked political and economic differences between the two contexts, in both cases we see how femifocal household patterns triggered by migration have opened up female social spaces and fostered sisterhood. Within highly mobile livelihoods then, sisterhood may provide the necessary stability and reliability to go on.

Acknowledgments

I thank all participants of the workshop on siblinghood at the University of Bayreuth in November 2009 for their stimulating and helpful comments. I want to especially thank Erdmute Alber and Sjaak van der Geest, the organizers of the workshop, for their highly inspiring enthusiasm and expertise throughout the workshop. Very insightful and important comments from Cati Coe, Erdmute Alber, Tatjana Thelen, and an anonymous reviewer significantly helped to enhance the paper. Monika Böck, Maren Rössler, Michael Schnegg, and David Sabean also gave elaborate and helpful comments on an earlier version of my paper, for which I am thankful.

Chapter 3

Kinship as Friendship

Brothers and Sisters in Kwahu, Ghana

Sjaak van der Geest

Siblingship and friendship have a paradoxical relationship. They are in one respect each other's antipode, but they also share common sentiments of belonging and affection. To paraphrase the French poet Jacques Delille, fate chooses your siblings; *you* choose your friends. Friendship seems voluntary, siblingship ascribed. "[Friendship] . . . evades definition: the way in which friendship acts to express fixity and fluidity in diverse social worlds is exciting and problematic for the people that practice friendship and for the social scientists that study it" (Killick and Desai 2010: 1). Friendship has in common with marriage that it is a voluntary bond, but it "lacks religious and legal grounding, rendering the creation, maintenance, and dissolution of friendship an essentially private, negotiable endeavor" (Tillmann-Healy 2003: 731).

Philosophers, psychologists, and also anthropologists have tried to point out the distinctive differences between marital love, sexual love, kinship, and friendship. Friendship stands apart from kinship bonds, as we have seen, because it is not framed by rules and rituals; is not based on common "contractual" interests such as economic security, income, and shared responsibility for children; and does not involve sexual attraction. Even though institutions like marriage and kinship may vary considerably across cultures and classes, friendship's distinctive difference seems to apply widely across social and cultural boundaries (see Adams and Allan 1998, Bell and Coleman 1999,

Desai and Killick 2010).[1] Its most outstanding distinction seems to be that it is *not* encased by social rules and religious sanctions. Of course, that appearance is an illusion; nothing can remain untouched by the conventions and restrictions of its surroundings. But comparatively, friendship appears to us as a relatively free attachment that is admired and cherished universally because of its disinterested and untainted character.[2]

The fact that friendship appears to escape the nets of society's regulations gives it an almost utopian status and makes it a phenomenon that presents an alternative to the Hobbesian world we live in. Friendship is seen as unselfish and disinterested and, therefore, does not need the formal rules that marriage requires. Because of its altruistic appearance, friendship is often portrayed as the purest form of love, almost a glimpse of a better world.[3]

And yet, kinship—and siblingship in particular—proves a favorite metaphor to express or engender friendship. The terms *brother* and *sister* are commonly used to emphasize the close emotional relationship between people who are not in any way related through biological kinship. David K. Jordan (1985) shows this attraction to kin terms in Chinese bonds of friendship, which he coins "sworn brotherhood." Rita Smith Kipp (1986) describes how lovers in Northern Sumatra, Indonesia, use sibling terminology to express their affection. "Lovers cast each other as siblings," the author summarizes in her conclusion. Auksuole Cepaitiene (2008) applies the metaphoric grasping of friendship in sibling terms to people who have together gone through moments of crisis and great danger. Finally, Reidar Aasgaard (2004), an exegete, analyzes the use of *brother* and *sister* in the letters of Saint Paul to early Christian communities. Being members of one religious minority group and sharing a common destiny is compared to being members of one family. That the concepts of friendship and kinship merge in these particular contexts is intriguing given the fact that scholars have exerted themselves separating and juxtaposing the very same concepts almost as mutually exclusive.

In this essay, I will unravel the sometimes overlapping, sometimes opposing appearances of kinship and friendship, based on ethnographic observations and conversations in a rural Ghanaian community. By looking at kinship from the perspective of friendship, I intend to shed more light on sibling experiences—a largely neglected area in the once so popular study of kinship.

SIBLINGHOOD IN EARLY KINSHIP STUDIES

In the ethnographies of the forties, fifties, and sixties of the previous century, when kinship took a central position, brothers and sisters only received cursory attention next to husband-wife, grandparents-grandchildren, and so on. Moreover, the picture was a rather static one, as was the anthropological mode at that time. The authors attempted to sketch the "structural" character of the relationship based on what people *said* and on what, according to them, *ought to be* rather than on what they observed. I do not, however, agree with the rather easy critique of some present-day anthropologists who disregard structural functionalists for their static perspective. They were aware that they were describing rules rather than realities. Meyer Fortes (1970: 3), for example, wrote, "When we describe structure, we are already dealing with general principles far removed from the complicated skein of behavior, feelings, beliefs, &c, that constitute the tissue of actual social life. We are, as it were, in the realm of grammar and syntax, not of the spoken word." The insights that structural functionalism produced in the first half of the twentieth century should never be thrown overboard, but rather included in our attempts to understand the complex and whimsical nature of daily life. This chapter tries to sketch these intertwinements and contradictions of rule and reality—grammar and "spoken word."

Meyer Fortes (1969) devoted more attention to siblings than most of his contemporaries.[4] He did this in a collection of articles on "Kinship and Social Order." His discussion revolves largely around juridical concepts such as rights, property, inheritance, and succession. Most of his examples are taken from his research in Ghana in the 1940s among the Asante, an Akan society that is closely related to the Kwahu where I started my fieldwork more than twenty-five years later. Fortes shifted his attention to the Asante after his extensive fieldwork among the Tallensi in northern Ghana. About siblingship in the Asante family, he observed, "The often quoted proverb 'The lineage is like an army but your own mother's child is your true sibling [that is, your closest kinsman]' expresses pithily the Ashanti ideal of siblingship. The unity of the sibling group is exemplified in the norms of residence;

their solidarity is stressed in the assumption that absolute loyalty and unrestricted confidence and intimacy distinguish the relations of siblings, irrespective of sex, by contrast with the conjugal relationship, and their jural equivalence is shown in the rules governing inheritance and succession" (Fortes 1969: 172). Those rules stipulate that inheritance and succession do not pass from parent to child but from sibling to sibling: "Full matri-siblings are 'one person,' 'of one womb,' a corporate unit in the narrowest sense, and sibling succession expresses the recognition of this indivisible corporate identity of the sibling group in opposition to the total matrilineage" (Fortes 1969: 175). But, concluding his discussion, he makes an important reservation that reveals his awareness of the relativity of these strict kinship rules: "[Behind these rules and restrictions] lies the assumption that siblings as autonomous persons are rivals beneath the surface of their amity" (Fortes 1969: 176).

Interestingly, authors of that period who did write about siblings in their ethnographies usually provided cases of conflicts between brothers and sisters, since peaceful and harmonious relations do not constitute a proper "case" in the eyes of most anthropologists. Nevertheless, the final analysis of such conflict cases usually resulted in a reconciliatory conclusion, thus honoring the harmony principle of functionalism. Conflicts were only temporary crises that eventually led to a reintegration or reshuffling of the conflicting parties and a strengthening of the overall kinship system.

My own fieldwork (Bleek 1975)[5] in Kwahu, Ghana, was an attempt to question or at least nuance the harmonious and somewhat static perception of family life in the context of Akan society. Looking back, I may have been too harsh and too pessimistic in my zeal to disprove the idyll of a firm underlying unity, but I still hold on to my view that the family I stayed with was riddled with conflicts and jealousy, also between siblings, that rarely were allowed to appear in the open. I will return to this research later on in my text.

After the 1960s, kinship largely disappeared from ethnography, at least as a central interest. The focus shifted to politics, economy, religion, indigenous knowledge, and symbolism. Kinship studies became the *pars pro toto* of an outdated type of anthropology, and the complex kinship classifications and terminologies were jokingly referred to as "kinship algebra." It was only in the late 1990s that kinship returned to being a focus of anthropology, not as a structured system of descent and alliance, but as a process and a lived experience of belonging (see, for example, Carsten 1997, 2000). But in spite of this fresh look at kinship, the mutual belonging of siblings was still largely overlooked—an enigmatic blind spot, if one takes into account the metaphoric charm of siblings mentioned before and the prominent presence of brothers and sisters in drama,[6] Biblical stories,[7] novels,[8] fairy tales (Clerkx 2009), and movies.[9]

Now, more than fifty years after Fortes's work in Asante, conversations with people in the same town where I carried out my earlier research show an extremely diverse picture of brother-sister relationships. It has become impossible to speak of brothers and sisters in general terms. Experiences of love, jealousy, and animosity concerning brothers and sisters differ depending on issues such as age, filial position, migration, economic dependence, life stage, personal character, and biography.

FIELDWORK

My initial fieldwork in 1971 in a rural Kwahu town in Ghana explored the dynamic and conflictual character of kinship and family life (Bleek 1975). The research was carried out in one matrilineage (*abusua*) of about a hundred and fifty members, of whom forty-five had died in the two previous generations but were very much present in the conversations I held with forty-six living members. In total, I "collected" seventy life histories, some extensive, others rather brief. I lived six months in the house of the family head, where I observed what happened, from the drudge of daily life to the more dramatic political and ceremonial events that are bound to take place in the house of a family head (formal greetings of travelers, lodging complaints, and settling conflicts and other cases). The direction of the research was determined by a case that involved the family head himself. Inspired by Van Velzen's (1967) "extended case method," my Ghanaian friend and I used that case as a starting point for our study. It led us to three "hot issues" that caused considerable friction and conflict in that Kwahu family: marriage and divorce, death and inheritance, and witchcraft accusations. In all of these, siblings played prominent but ambiguous roles.

One and a half years later, I returned to the same family for research on sexual relationships and birth control (Bleek 1976). My quite intimate knowledge of and good relationship with most members of the family helped me to pursue this rather delicate topic of "shameful" practices such as secret sex and abortion. Siblingship as such was not the subject of that research and did not present itself as a relevant concept except for the fact that brothers and sisters sometimes helped one another in love affairs.

I did not go back to Ghana until twenty-one years later when I started a research project on experiences of growing old and care for older people. In the years that followed, I developed an interest in several other—often underexposed—aspects of Kwahu culture. Brother-sister relationships were added to that list after a discussion with Erdmute Alber, which drew my attention to this touching, yet largely forgotten, domain of kinship and social belonging.

I reread my early fieldwork notes and publications and held conversations with twelve people on brother and sister relationships during visits to Kwahu in 2007 and 2008. I also asked fifty-seven students of the local senior high school to write an essay about their relationship with a brother or a sister.[10] The main body of my "data" derives from this more recent work and confirms the diverse and highly ambiguous nature of the way that brothers and sisters relate to one another.

All conversations were held in the rural town of Kwahu-Tafo, which has a population of approximately six thousand according to the 2000 Census. Kwahu-Tafo is an "average" Kwahu town. Most of the inhabitants are—at least part-time—farmers. Many, women in particular, run a small store selling daily necessities. The town has electricity and running water, but only a few households benefit from the latter. Wells and rain still constitute the main supplies of water. Stores sell sachets with drinking water. There are about ten different primary schools, public as well as private, and about fifteen different Christian churches in the town. A mosque is in the *Zongo*, the Islamic quarter.

Kwahu people belong to Ghana's about ten million Akan[11] and have a matrilineal kinship system. Traditionally, and as explained by Fortes for the Asante, marriage is less binding than lineage membership, which may cause considerable ambivalence in people who have to negotiate between their marital partner and the matrilineage (*abusua*), including their siblings.[12]

THE DIVERSITY OF SIBLING RELATIONS

To explore the intertwining of experiences concerning siblingship and friendship, we first need ethnographic light on the variety in siblingship. The question as to whom one loved most or to whom one was closest (sister or brother?) prompted lively discussions among friends. Their answers, including detailed stories about childhood, adolescence, and life after marriage, provided an extremely diverse picture. It all depended, most emphasized, on character and behavior, on who happens to be around, and on age differences. Moreover, the English terms *brother* and *sister*, as well as the local term *onua* (used for both male and female siblings), were problematic. In the Akan language Twi, the terms are also used for cousins, primarily first cousins but also those who are more remote. People do not always make a sharp distinction between brothers and sisters from the same mother and others. If cousins grow up in the same house, the distinction may not be made at all, which complicates *and* enlightens the discussion, as we will see further on. I will attempt to point at a number of "trends" in the conversations we held.

Brother to Brother, Sister to Sister

Several women said they liked their sister(s) more than their brother(s), because as sisters they have more in common. They enjoyed conversing with their sisters about problems and issues that affect them as women and mothers—for example, bringing up children, kitchen affairs, clothes, finances, and marital concerns. In the same vein, men said they had more in common with their brothers and preferred to discuss matters with them. One man said, "Being a man, you can discuss every problem you have with your brother but not with your sister. You take your brother as your friend. Moreover, sisters travel with their husband to another town, so you may not have contact with them. So, to me, a brother is more important than a sister." Both men and women remarked that they shared secrets with their brothers and sisters, respectively. "Sharing secrets" was a favorite definition of friendship by an elder whom I will quote extensively toward the end of this essay.

Having common interests and competencies is also likely to develop into helping one another in tasks that are gender specific. One woman cited how her mother received help from her sister in bringing up two of her children. Or should we rather say that her mother helped her sister by giving her two of her children? "Two of my mother's sisters could not have children; one of them took care of me and my sister. We stayed with her from our infancy until we got married. It is not so long ago that I came to stay here [she moved to her mother's house after her husband had died]." Both men and women emphasized that from childhood onwards, games and other activities tended to become more and more gender specific. Separation of the sexes occurs also in the work that boys and girls carry out in the house, although that distinction is not always strict. Girls are more likely to sweep, wash cooking utensils and clothes, and carry garbage to the "boiler" (dunghill) at the outskirts of the town. Boys are more engaged in weeding, carrying heavy loads, and activities involving domestic animals.

Sleeping arrangements are another factor contributing to the demarcation between brothers and sisters. One man said, "My mother had eight children, only one of whom was a girl. We the boys always slept together in one room. Our sister always slept with our mother." And he continued, "As girls are closer to the mother, they sometimes act as 'informants' and report everything the boys do to the mother." To summarize, growing up in Kwahu society, as everywhere, is a process of "genderization" that slowly drives boys and girls apart and widens the gap between brothers and sisters, and, according to some, leads to a closer relationship between siblings of the same sex.

This is, however, only one side of the coin. Common interests, as sisters or brothers may have, could also lead to competition and feelings of jealousy if one is more successful than the other (see also Pauli, this volume). In fact, conflicts and envy among sisters was a common observation that was raised during our conversations. Here is an excerpt of one such conversation between three men and myself:

> P: Sisters in the same house often quarrel. Especially when they get children and the children begin to grow, each of them is concerned about her own children. This causes deterioration in their relationship. Men are not like that.

Figure 3.1   Sisters Doing the Dishes

Figure 3.2   Two Brothers, Senior and Junior, Carrying Garbage to the Dunghill

Sj: Why are men not like that? Are they not concerned about their own children?

P: Men are able to cope, but three sisters from the same mother staying in the same house; not a week will pass without them quarrelling.

Sj: (to M) do you agree with what P is saying?

M: Yes, I second him. Women staying in the same house, whether they are from the same mother or not, they will quarrel and gossip.

Sj: (to B) What do you say about this?

B: What they are saying is true. When their children are fighting, each mother will defend her own child . . . There will hardly be peace when women (sisters) stay together.

Women bear long grudges, another man said, while men make up after quarrels. Another man remarked that the relationship between sisters turns sour more easily than between brothers. One may be inclined to discard these as typical male chauvinistic views, but women said similar things. To quote one of them, "If there are many sisters, there are many quarrels. They quarrel. Everyone knows how women are. If my brother gives me a cloth, the other will complain that he did not give one to her." Jealousy may start at a young age if one sister (or brother) is more loved by her or his parents or teacher than another. One man remembered, "Perhaps I am more absent from the house than my brother and I am punished. My brother does not go out much, so he is called to do a lot of things, even though I am the senior [!]. If such a thing happens, I will begin to hate him. There will be suspicion and jealousy. [He continued with a similar example in a school context]." The remark about being "senior" is important. Brothers and sisters have a strong awareness of being older or younger. The younger should "respect," or show deference, to the older (*ɔpanyin*). If for some reason the younger commands more respect than the older (for example because of higher education, more success in life, or being more popular), the relationship is under stress. In his survey on child training practices in Ghana, Barrington Kaye (1962: 159) also found the concept of seniority to be very strong throughout the country. Although younger children in Asante may enjoy certain privileges from their parents, they are subordinate to their older brothers and sisters and must help them with household chores such as sweeping and carrying water. In return, the juniors expect their older siblings to give them food or money to help them pay their school fees. "Young children are taught to respect their older siblings" (Kaye 1962: 164). Kaye starts his chapter on siblings with a quotation from an unrevealed source: "The first-born is regarded as the head of other children in the house; he has the right to punish or reprimand a younger brother or sister" (Kaye 1962: 159). That sense of responsibility for younger siblings starts early in life: older children take care of younger brothers and sisters, carry them, and give them instructions.

It is only a small step from jealousy, mentioned before, to accusations and suspicions of witchcraft.[13] Nearly all my informants agreed that women are more likely to practice witchcraft. However, it did not always become clear if their supposed witchcraft was mainly targeted toward their sisters or relatives in general. During my first research (Bleek 1975), I discovered a dense network of witchcraft accusations within one (extended) family. Nearly every member of the family was involved as accuser, accused witch, or suspected victim of witchcraft. I categorized the relations between the "witches" and their "victims." Out of a total of fifty-four accusations, twelve referred to supposed witchcraft between siblings and ten between the children of sisters (who call one another "brother" and "sister"). I also looked at the relationship between accuser and accused (which seemed to me a better indication of a strained relationship). The highest number (twelve) were children of sisters. I did not mark the sex of the accusers and accused, but in general women were far more accused of witchcraft than men.

In conclusion, sharing interests and having common ideas and experiences at first appears as a favorable condition that fosters a close relationship between siblings of the same sex, particularly among sisters. However, that very condition is also a potential risk that may disturb the relationship and turn intimate siblings into rivals for the same material or social benefits. Numerous proverbs, which mostly allude to witchcraft, emphasize that closeness is inherently ambiguous and liable to turn into animosity and envy. One of them goes, "It is the insect in your own cloth that bites you" (*Aboa a ɔhyɛ wo ntoma mu, na ɔka wo*). It is precisely because of this risky closeness that most of the people I talked to thought that the greater distance between brothers and sisters gave more room for love and life-long affection than relations between siblings of the same sex.

Brother to Sister, Sister to Brother

Most women spoke in warm terms about their brothers, especially those who stated emphatically that having sisters in one house meant quarrelling. They liked their brothers because they showed more willingness to help them, and their relationships were free from rivalry and jealousy. One woman said, "Men are closer to me than women. If there is any job to be done, the men will do it. If there is a problem in the house and the men have no money, they will offer advice, which brings peace to the family. . . . When the men saw that this house was small and they found it difficult to get a place to sleep, they brought money and extended the house." One older woman was very outspoken about her preference for brothers. She had been drawn toward men throughout her life. No wonder that this lady preferred her brothers to her sisters. "These women, when you tell them, 'Let us do this or that,' they will say, 'No,' knowing very well it would be the best thing to do. If something needs to be done, why don't you ask a man? Women disagree among each other. Honestly, I like my brothers better than my sisters. When I open my box and bring out my old photographs, you will see that many of them are my brothers and me. I never took a photograph with my sisters [she had three sisters]." She remembered the special affection she had for her uncle's (*Wɔfa*; mother's brother's) son who came to stay with her mother and became like a brother, although he would also qualify as a good marriage partner. "There was no difference between him and my real brothers. A lot of people thought we were from the same mother and father. I was close to him because he listened to what I said and I also listened to what he said. When he was going to Accra to work, I gave him eight shillings [at that time the transport fare to Accra was four shillings]. I told him, he should inform me whenever he needed money. As for men, I loved them more than women." Another woman, around sixty-five years old, also expressed a strong preference for brothers: "Women only think of their own children [they do not think of the entire family]. Men will never go to a 'fetish priest'[14] or to a spiritual church to pray for their own children only to become successful in life. We the women do go to the 'fetish priest' to get a good husband for their children. Men will never do that." A sister's love for her brother can be intertwined with rivalry toward her sisters. One man told me that his mother was the first of three sisters and one brother. At that time it was the custom that a sister's son would inherit from his mother's brother (*wɔfa*). His mother's youngest sister then tried to become very close to her brother, hoping that one of her sons would inherit from her brother. She succeeded in her plan, even though according to the tradition a son of the oldest sister should have priority.[15]

Only one man (who had been married four times and had about fifteen children) mentioned the matrilineal principle as a reason sisters are more important to a man than brothers: "It is more important to have sisters because they continue the family line. It is my sister's children who will inherit me, so I am more interested in them." He had—for that reason—sponsored the education of sons of several sisters. I asked him who would take care of him when he grew old. He replied that his own children would, provided he had taken good care of them. During the conversation he shifted his position somewhat and admitted that his preference for sisters was somewhat "theoretical"—more based on family interests than on his own. Continuation of the *abusua* as a reason for men to be close to their sisters proved indeed somewhat abstract. When I asked one of my personal friends about it, he replied, "I do not think about what will happen after my death; however, if there is any help I can give to my sisters and her children, I will do so if I have the means." Brothers usually remain very concerned about the well-being of their sister after she marries. "If the husband of your sister beats her or causes any other damage, she will come to her family house and ask for help. That is the reason that men may intervene when their sisters are not well treated in marriage." Conversely, if the marriage of a sister is "too successful" and draws her to her husband's side, away from her brother, the brother may decide to intervene to pull her back into the *abusua*. The conflict that started my research in 1971 is a case in point. The relationship between a woman, Oforiwa, and her husband Osei was very close. "We did everything together," Osei told me. When a conflict erupted between Osei and the (classificatory) brother of his wife, she chose her husband's side, to her brother's dismay and anger. When she suddenly died two years later, her brother refused to bury her since she was "no longer his sister." A respected older man gave the following comment: "Oforiwa made the big mistake of supporting her husband against her brother. This is unforgivable. Even if the brother was completely wrong, she should still support him against her husband" (Bleek 1975: 77). Brothers' attitude of dedication to their sisters starts at a very young age. Boys defend their sisters and fight for them when they are wronged or falsely accused of something. Brothers may also find it difficult to accept their sister's boyfriend, particularly the first one. They experience this as some kind of betrayal and the beginning of losing her.

Sisters show their appreciation for their brothers by subtle services—for example, washing their clothes or cooking food for them. When a boy becomes interested in girls, his sister may help him to approach a certain girl by mediating for him.

There are several complicating factors, however. The age difference between a brother and a sister may have a profound influence on the relationship that develops. During my conversation with three men (quoted previously), it turned out that all three had only one sister. In two cases, the sister was much younger and the two men never felt very close to that sister. They were too far apart. When they faced problems and wanted to discuss these with somebody, their sister was still a child. In one case, however, the sister was much older and became like a mother for the brother. The real mother was often away, staying with her husband in a farming village and leaving the running of the house to her grown-up daughter and her older brothers. I know both the man and his sister very well and observed that they are still very close. The man's wife is staying far away, as a teacher, and he spends a great deal of the day with his sister. He takes some of his meals from her and now even spends the night in her house.

Conversely, as we have seen at the onset of this section, men are believed to have more financial means and are expected to help their sisters when they are in need. It is a disgrace if a man who is well off refuses to support his sister, as is expressed in an old Highlife song by Alex Konadu. A woman complains about her brother's refusal to help her. Her name, she says, is connected to him for nothing; he sleeps on his money without giving her anything. People mock at her saying, "This woman is the sister of a rich man." The song is a negative confirmation that brothers are supposed to support their sister.

Marriage often entails a breaking point in the relationship of siblings, mainly for two reasons. The interests of the married person shift from his or her siblings to the new partner and particularly his or her children. In addition, the marriage may involve a geographical move as well, so the brother or sister will be around no more. Several of my friends indicated that traveling and residing elsewhere put an end to their close relationship with a brother or sister. That emotional shift during the life cycle was well expressed by one woman: "We women, as soon as we grow and marry, we begin to think about our children. We unite with them and tear ourselves from our sisters and brothers." But that move away may be reversed after some time; the same woman continued, "Disunity begins to set in when children grow. At that time, we again become closer to our brothers." The reason for that return to the brother is, as we have seen, that brothers are believed to be more prepared to think outside their nuclear family and to resume their role as *wɔfa* (sister's brother). Moreover, sisters may indeed be eager to benefit from their brother's generosity. But suspicion remains on both sides. A proverb goes, "If you say your sister loves you, wait until her children have grown" (*Sɛ wose wo nuabea ne wo ka a, ma ne mma nyin na hwɛ*). The implication of the proverb is that the sister is likely to still favor her children over her brother.

Where the close relationship between a brother and a sister does survive the sister's marriage, another problem may turn up. The brother may find himself caught between his sister and his wife and fall "victim" to another type of rivalry. The "pure" relation between brother and sister thus becomes entangled in competing claims and interests and will force the brother to choose between one and the other.

We should not take the brother-sister relationship too idealistically, therefore. It is also a practical affair that finds its origin in very mundane circumstances. The most decisive—and most obvious—is the presence or availability of a brother or sister; an intense and lasting brother-sister love is likely to occur where the two happen to be in each other's vicinity. That idea is beautifully expressed in a proverb: "The sister or brother of a bird is the one sitting on the same branch" (*Anomaa nua ne nea ɔne no da dua krɔ so*). One of my friends provided another translation, making the application even more direct: "The sister or brother of a bird is the one sleeping in the same bed."[16]

CONCLUDING: SIBLINGSHIP AND FRIENDSHIP, SIBLINGSHIP AS FRIENDSHIP

During a long conversation, an elder in Kwahu-Tafo compared sib-lingship, marriage, and friendship as follows:

> The inscription on my house reads: *Onipa nua ne nea ɔne no ka* [A person's brother is the one who loves him]. If a brother does not love you there is nothing you can do. A person who loves you should be everything to you. No matter how a brother may be, you can't do away with him (*Wɔyɛ oo, wɔnyɛ oo, worentumi mpopa*). Whether a brother is good or bad, he will succeed you in the future, but a friend never will. At the same time, the love between friends can be deeper than the love between brothers. I have a friend and the love between us is more special than the one between my brother and me. I am able to disclose all my secrets to him (*Mitumi ne no ka atrimu sɛm*), something I don't do with my brother. I scarcely converse with my brother and at times our conversation ends in a quarrel. My friend and I are able to share one bed, eat together and even bathe with one bucket of water, something I don't do with my brother. All this is done out of love (*Ne nyinaa yɛ ɔdɔ*).
>
> Love in friendship is the purest (*Adamfoɔ mu dɔ no na ɛyɛ ɔdɔ ankasa*) because friends always pray that the other won't die or fall into trouble so that their friendship will last a long time. But it is the wish of some people that their brothers die so that they can take their belong-ings. Indeed, there is no pure love among brothers. Love in friendship is very deep and there is happiness in it.
>
> Friendship usually starts casually. It starts first with greetings which will later on develop into a conversation. This goes on for some time. Then it develops into full friendship. Friendship may end when one leaves the other and travels to a distant place. But even when such a thing happens, friends are able to maintain their friendship by sending messages to one another. Friendship can last till death. I have seen such a friendship. I had one myself. . . .
>
> Let me tell you about my own friendship. I saw that my friend did not like gossiping and that he respected himself (*obu ne ho*). I also saw that he was hard working. These qualities attracted me. Ever since we started our friendship we have been getting along well. We plan how we can look after our wives. My wife is aware of all these qualities in him so she receives him warmly whenever he is here and she feels happy when he is around. When we were young we used to help each other in clearing our farms (*yedi nnɔboa*). Now that I am old, I can't go to farm,

Figure 3.3 Brothers or Friends?

but we visit one another frequently for conversation. When we meet we share our meals together. Even when I am not around and there is a problem with the children my wife contacts him for help. . . . A friend is someone with whom you share secrets.[17]

The elder singled out friendship as a virtue that is more precious than siblingship. What makes his treatise on kinship and friendship most valuable is his eloquent reuniting of these two distinctive types of human bonding. The opening line of his response to my questions—"A person's brother is the one who loves him"—captures the point of my argument.[18] Siblingship is more than biological linkage, *and* friendship and love make two people like brothers. The distinction "voluntary" versus "ascribed" is too schematic. The experience of siblingship could be more a matter of choice and personal preference than the grammar of kinship wants us to believe. Friendship and siblingship become intermingled in various ways. Robert Brain (1977: 16) suggests "that all kin relations within our kinship group are based on friendship and personal choice. One chooses this or that uncle, this or that cousin, even this or that brother or sister to be friendly with." In an intriguing discussion of Meyer Fortes's *Kinship and the Social Order* (1969), Julian Pitt-Rivers (1973) picks out the term *amity*, which Fortes chose to distinguish kinship from other types of relationship. *Amity* stands for "the axiom of prescriptive altruism" (Fortes's words). Pitt-Rivers then points out that *amity* is just another term for *friendship*, which is not prescriptive in the sense that altruism is among kin. In other words, according to Pitt-Rivers, "Fortes has chosen to define the essence of kinship by appealing to the very concept of what it is not" (90). But instead of rejecting the term for that reason (failing to achieve its mission), Pitt-Rivers welcomes it because "it offers the possibility of placing the notion of kinship in a wider framework and of escaping from the polemics concerning its relationship to physical reproduction" (90). Fortes was right, after all, highlighting the amity that is expected between members of one family. Why? Pitt-Rivers explains, "Despite the common opposition of the terms kinship and friendship, there is room for variants partaking in the properties of both, between the pole of kinship, inflexible, involuntary, immutable, established by birth and subject to the pressures of 'the political-jural domain' (in Fortes' words) and the pole of friendship, pure and simple, which is its contrary in each of these ways. All these 'amiable' relations imply a moral obligation to feel—or at least to feign—sentiments which commit the individual to actions of altruism, to generosity" (90). I understand this as follows: Pitt-Rivers suggests that a rigid analytical distinction between friendship and kinship is not helpful to understand how kinship works. Amity—or friendship—enters the domain of kin relations. "True kinship" is not determined by birth but by morality: voluntary altruism and generosity.

Another significant connection between siblingship and friendship is that sibling terms are used to speak to friends and lovers, as we have seen earlier on in this essay (Aasgaard 2004, Cepaitiene 2008, Jordan 1985, Kipp 1986). Mac Marshall argues against an exclusively biological concept of kinship, based on his work in Truk society in Micronesia. He uses the subtle transformations from friendship into siblingship as a case in point. In their belief, "persons who take care of and nurture each other prove their kinship in the process" (Marshall 1977: 657).

Janet Carsten (2000: 73), citing Marshall, remarks that "created siblings are better siblings than natural siblings." It is worthwhile to quote Marshall more fully: "Consanguineal siblings are . . . born into an inherently ambivalent relationship, a matter that may account for the restraint that surrounds their interaction. Created sibling relationships are not only as good as natural ones, they are potentially better. They are an improvement on nature in the sense that they allow for the purest expression of 'brotherly love' in Trukese culture" (Marshall 1977: 649). The paradox is that people choose kinship terms to express love and affection, apparently assuming that the truest love is found in kinship, such as between siblings. But, at the same time, they recognize that a voluntarily chosen relationship is more precious and carries deeper emotional satisfaction than one that has been thrown on them. It would have been more "correct," one could argue, to use terms of love and friendship to express dear kinship relations. That "more correct" metaphoric terminology, however, has nowhere been observed, as far as I know. Carsten (2000: 73) referred to the same paradox when she wrote, "relatedness based solely on voluntarily created ties of affection is closer to an ideal of kinship than that based on biological reproduction."

The bond between siblings, and between brothers and sisters in particular, seems closest to the purity and endurance of friendship ties that people engage in during their life. Although the relationship is ascribed, as it is based on kinship, it resembles the friendship that develops independently of kinship rules and obligations. Friendship is free from interests. Reciprocity is not counted in friendship even though it cannot exist without it (see Killick 2010). In the same way, it is believed, brothers and sisters find themselves in a position where unconditional mutual support and love can exist and grow.

Friendship, usually, is between persons of the same gender, and it is very different from love between a man and a woman that is likely to become a sexual relationship and—eventually—also an economic union, a kind of contract. What is remarkable in the brother-sister relationship is that it is a cross-gender bond without, in most cases, any sexual implication.[19] In that sense, it is indeed "pure" love.

Finally, the brother-sister bond lasts a lifetime and passes through the various life stages of people, as the elder said about friendship. It may change its character along the way without losing its fundamental mutual affection and dedication. Unlike the cross-generational relationships that occur only during a period of one's life, the connection between a brother and a sister remains from beginning to end.

Like friendship, a warm and strong relationship between a brother and a sister is an opportunity one must grasp in life. Like culture in general, the friendship of the sibling is not simply given, handed down, and dictated by biology, tradition, or an older generation; it is a choice that people make—a chance that they take and develop throughout their lifetime.

ACKNOWLEDGMENTS

I thank the participants of the workshop "Brother- and Sisterhood from an Anthropological Perspective" (Bayreuth 2009) and the editors of this volume for their comments on earlier versions of this essay, in particular Cati Coe. To pursue the metaphor that I discussed before, the ideas expressed in this essay are the fruit of many years of moving with friends in Kwahu-Tafo, friends who became like brothers and sisters. Four of them need to be mentioned by name: Anthony Yaw Obeng Boamah, Benjamin D. Boadu, Patrick Atuobi, and Monica Amoakoa. I dedicate this essay to the last two; they presented me with a model of life-long brother-sister love.

PART 2

SIBLINGSHIP AS LIFE-LONG EXCHANGE

CHAPTER 4

WITHIN THE THICKET OF INTERGENERATIONAL SIBLING RELATIONS

A CASE STUDY FROM NORTHERN BENIN

Erdmute Alber

Acting as a brother or a sister provides people with rights, but it also creates obligations and role expectations. Experiencing the powerful decisions of siblings (or parents' siblings) can be a painful experience as well. But at the same time, siblings can maintain close and warm mutual relations, as often mentioned in the literature, as well as remain resources to be mobilized in difficult moments of the life course. Thus sibling relations have to be seen as integral and powerful parts of the web of kinship that were often overlooked in the classical anthropological literature. And, as I want to show, it is sometimes sibling relations that make the web of kinship, as it was named by Meyer Fortes, a real thicket.

In this chapter, I analyze the intergenerational conflict prompted by a girl named Djamila that happened recently among rural and urban Baatombu in the Republic of Benin.[1] The dynamics of that conflict are not understandable if one does not take various relations between siblings into account. This is why I think that an analysis of the particular conflict with a special focus on the various sibling relations could be useful for a better understanding of what it means to be a brother or a sister in northern Benin and, further on, siblingship in general.[2]

I use Djamila's story in order to outline one key argument: that relations between siblings are not only part of horizontal relations in the web of kinship. Rather, they are of major importance in understanding the dynamics of intergenerational relations as well. One of the reasons for this is that an important element that constitutes relations between siblings is the interaction between people and their siblings' children. In the anthropological literature, this relationship was mainly raised as an issue by looking at the mother's brother and his relationship to a sister's son or daughter.[3] But there are also other constellations—for example, women may entrust their children to their sisters when they work. Or, in patrilineal households in which brothers live together with their wives and children, their sons and daughters often grow up together as siblings. Taking care or responsibility for the children of siblings—or, as is a central social norm among the Baatombu in northern Benin, fostering siblings' children—is an essential part of the relationship between siblings. It gives sibling relations an intergenerational dimension. Of course, the opposite is also true, as the conflict around Djamila will show: neglecting, maltreating, or denying responsibility for relatedness with the children of siblings leads to conflicts between siblings in which they renegotiate the perceptions and norms of siblingship.

My argument of the relevance of sibling relations for intergenerational dynamics is based on the assumption that whenever people share their lifetimes and understand themselves as being related to one another, their perception of kinship always provides a plurality of role expectations that they could or have to perform (or deny playing). Women are, simultaneously, (grand)mothers, wives, and sisters. Men have rights and obligations as (grand)fathers, husbands, and brothers. These different kinship roles are linked to one another. The way of being and acting as a sister can influence the way in which one performs as a wife. Looking at siblingship and its entanglement with other kinship roles is thus of importance to understand not only what it means to be a brother or a sister but also what it means to be an uncle or a loyal husband. I wish to argue that the different kinship roles of a spouse, a parent, and a sibling should be understood as interlinked.[4] It is this multitude of roles, among other factors, that creates and accelerates conflicts. On the other hand, this multitude also includes the possibility of deciding preferences, which means that people are not reduced on one single role. In the case of a bad marriage, to give only one example, sibling relations could become of increasing importance (see also van der Geest, this volume).

My approach is the extended case study following Max Gluckman (1961) and Jaap Van Velsen (1967), who theorized about how far the analysis of one specific case could provide answers and knowledge about general patterns. Additionally, I was inspired by Michael Burawoy's argument (1998) that this method, if combined with reflexivity concerning the role of the researcher, is especially useful in understanding political and social conflicts and class differentiations. As will become clear when telling Djamila's story, I am not only a researcher but also a deeply involved person with a social and kinship role in the urban and rural social fields I am analyzing here. My involvement in the case in question makes reflections about my own role and my interventions especially necessary. However, following Burawoy as well as Gerd Spittler's notion of "participant observation as a means of thick participation" (2001), I am confident that thick participation with a high degree of reflexivity generates insights one could not have had by remaining distant and neutral in the field.

In Djamila's story, as in general among the Baatombu, the fostering of children is another key issue that is closely intertwined with siblingship. Therefore I will give a brief introduction to the practices of fosterage and their relation to siblingship before coming to the story itself.

FOSTER PRACTICES AND SIBLINGSHIP

Before the arrival of French colonialism, almost all children among the Baatombu in northern Benin were fostered by people other than their biological parents. Even if the fostering rate has decreased, from about 90 percent of children at the beginning of the twentieth century to about 25 to 35 percent today, the percentage of children who do not grow up with their biological parents still remains high and will probably continue to be so (Alber 2004a; Alber, Martin, and Häberlein 2011). About two-thirds of the fostered children are living with brothers or sisters of their parents.[5]

Nowadays, different forms of fosterage can be observed, such as the fostering of village boys and girls by urban relatives in order to send them to school (Alber 2010) or the fostering of children who are expected to perform specific kinds of work—for instance, as cattle herders (Martin 2007) or food sellers. In villages, "kinship fostering" (Goody 1982) is still frequent. This means that children are fostered by relatives without any special economic or social reason given except that fostering is a way of linking kin. There are permanent forms of fostering as well as temporary ones (Alber 2003).

The importance of sibling relations in foster arrangements was a key finding in my quantitative work in three Baatombu villages. In these villages, about 65 percent of the foster parents are siblings of a child's mother or father. In the urban area, too, siblingship is an important factor in foster relations. As in the rural areas, there are also many brothers and sisters of children's parents who act as foster parents and host the children of their siblings in their households. Additionally, there is a new kind of fosterage that is gaining in importance—namely, the fostering of younger siblings from the rural areas by their elder brothers or sisters who already live in urban households. This is a kind of relation that I did not find within rural areas. This new type of foster relation, which could be interpreted as increasing the importance of sibling relations in the context of urbanization and rural-urban migration, is due to a sense of responsibility on the part of young urban adults toward their (still rural) younger siblings. Because they have left the villages and established themselves in the cities while their younger siblings attend village schools, they want to assist their siblings in making their own careers. As the rural parents cannot contribute to the younger siblings' mobility, successful older siblings take their brothers or sisters to live in their households (see also Obendiek, this volume).

This happens especially if the elder siblings have been pioneers in their families concerning their careers, and if they have gained access to relatively good economic positions in the cities, whatever the reason for that social climbing was. They feel that their duty as sisters or brothers is to help their younger siblings make a career similar to theirs. But they explain this behavior not only as a brotherly duty but also as an investment in the future. For I was told that, because the younger siblings would have been prepared to have good employment in the cities, they would, in the future, no longer need assistance from their older siblings in moments of crisis. Taking them into the town and their own households thus protects the older siblings from future demands. It is in this direction that new forms of rural-urban foster-age, based on a sense of responsibility within the sibling group, have developed recently. However, I would not take these responsibilities toward younger and economically weaker siblings as an example of the unity of the sibling group. Rather, these dynamics are developing because of increasing social and economic inequalities due to rapid urbanization. One effect is that sibling cohorts are more and more confronted with remarkable differentiation in education, access to economic wealth, and life chances that they have to deal with across their life course.

Forms and types of foster arrangements have changed and continue to change over time. Another very recent development, also due to rapid urbanization, is the rise of new types of rural-urban mobility of children and youth—namely, the fact that rural Baatombu girls who do not attend schools are given to urban households in order to do household work. They are not seen as domestic workers, since they are not formally paid, but the urban family heads are expected to pay, after some time, for a dowry or an apprenticeship for the girls. This new kind of social arrangement is, as is the fostering of rural school children by their urban siblings, due to the emergence of a rising urban Baatombu middle class whose lifestyles differ widely from the rural households of their relatives but are nevertheless closely connected with them. They take some responsibility for their relatives but also take advantage of a rising economic differentiation. These arrangements are apparently relatively easily accepted by rural parents, since they offer some life chances for the girls (as, for example, learning French or urban habits) that cannot be achieved in the rural area. I met some girls in those arrangements, the majority of them expressing that they preferred to continue living in these arrangements rather than return to the villages. As these arrangements are relatively new, there are many conflicts around them concerning the social and economic expectations toward the adults as well as toward the girls themselves. I would interpret Djamila's case, however, as one example of these new arrangements, as in any particular case, with special complications.

In the majority of urban and rural Baatombu households, foster and biological children grow up side by side, considering themselves to be brothers and sisters. They share a day-to-day life in common, which in many cases comes to an abrupt end—for example, when a child is taken away by foster parents, when a child is returned to his or her biological parents, or when a child leaves one household and joins another in order to be able to go to school or to work there.

A Baatombu child hardly ever grows up with his or her biological sisters and brothers exclusively; the normal situation in urban as well as rural Baatombu households is that "full" siblings grow up along-side "half" siblings as well as foster brothers and sisters. Especially in urban households, the living conditions of different children often differ widely. Being a newcomer among strange and "new" siblings is a common experience for Baatombu children, and many children also experience, when coming into an urban household, becoming a "second-class" sibling who works in the household while the other children attend school. However, despite all the hardships and insta-bility of sibling relations because of sometimes abrupt changes, the case of Djamila will also show that these kinship practices allow for opportunities to meet hitherto unknown persons and develop lasting relations.

As I shall further discuss, rural and urban Baatombu households are deeply interconnected. During the life course, people are moving from rural to urban households and back, and children are frequently transferred. Foster relations as well as sibling relations connect house-holds in different socioeconomic situations with one another, as will become apparent in Djamila's story.

THE STORY OF DJAMILA

In Djamila's story, different sibling relations played a crucial role. They include Djamila's own siblings as well as those of her parents (includ-ing the anthropologist). The story also illustrates the multitude of kinship relations and tensions. So that the reader is not completely lost, I will give a brief summary of what happened before examining the perspectives of the key persons.

Djamila[6] is a young woman whom I first met in 2007, when she worked in Cotonou in the household of the sister of her mother's brother's wife. At that time, she was about fifteen years old. In this household of the in-laws of her mother's brother, she was not paid but worked all day as a domestic worker without being offered formal education or an apprenticeship. She tried to escape the situation by calling her maternal half-brother, Kpaasi, a student in Cotonou, and asking him to help her get out of the situation.[7]

Kpaasi is considered my foster son, since I have, for several years, taken on the financial responsibility for his professional education. When he told me about his nearly unknown sister, I was curious, so we visited Djamila several times in her household and let her tell us her story. This was also new for Kpaasi, since he had never spent time with her. Djamila expressed that she did not want to waste her time in the household of the in-laws of her uncle without learning anything, but that she wanted to get into a skilled trade, such as becoming a tailor, for example.

Before being sent to Cotonou, she had spent her childhood as a foster girl with her father's sister, but as she had been beaten and mal-treated there, she had run away. After that, she lived for a short time with an elder paternal half-sister; then Bio, her maternal uncle, took responsibility for her. He sent her into the family of his in-laws (his wife's sister). Convinced that she was being exploited, I asked Kpaasi to inform Bio, who was their common mother's brother, about the situation. Some months later, I spoke directly to Bio as well.

He told me about the pressures on him if he criticized his wife's sister for maltreating the girl. As well, he told me about his responsibility as the maternal uncle of Djamila, Kpaasi, and their siblings. He concluded that he would like to put Djamila into an apprenticeship in a town, but in a "neutral" place—that is, a place connected neither to the family of Djamila's father nor to his own. He explained that he could not take her into his own household without creating a conflict with his wife. Finally, my field assistant, Bake, offered to help him find a place for Djamila in Parakou, the city where she lived.

Some months later, I met Djamila in Bake's household. She was working nearby as an apprentice in a tailor's workshop. Another year later, she had to return to the house of her biological parents, since she had become pregnant in Parakou. Later, she delivered a baby of an unknown father and was diagnosed as HIV positive.

Her paternal uncle denied her any further help, and his wife's sister accused Kpaasi of having encouraged the girl to leave. Bake her-self refused to accept her any longer in her house. During the whole time, I had regular conversations with Djamila's biological mother, who always declared in a shy and modest way that she was worried about her daughter, but as it was her brother who put Djamila into the household of his in-laws, she had neither the power nor the right to help her. Currently, Djamila lives in the household of her biological parents, raising her child and looking for an opportunity to change her life.

This short version of the story, and especially its unhappy end, seems to confirm a prominent image that child-protection institutions such as *terre des homes* or *Save the Children* communicate about working children in Benin.[8] It is the image of children as victims who are sent by ignorant and often profit-oriented relatives (here, Bio) into urban households, without the protection of their parents. Normally, and in the image of these institutions, it is only the child-protection organizations that can help the children to get out of their situations. Therefore I had, when I met Djamila for the first time, the idea to contact one of these institutions in order to "save" her from the thicket of her relatives. But Djamila herself had already chosen a viable strategy. She searched for help within the web of kinship and called on her previously unknown brother Kpaasi. Thus she took the fact of being part of complex kinship relations as something that not only created the problem she was captured by but also was a means of getting out of it.

My analysis confirms Djamila's perception, which I learned through my discussions with her. I wish to show how these complex kinship relations, and especially the various sibling relations, led to the difficult situation she was in but at the same time provided pathways out. However, my ex-post analysis not only follows this perception of the conflict; I also acted according to it. I came into the conflict as an anthropologist who was doing field research on rural-urban relations between Baatombu households, and one of my best contacts in the field, my foster son Kpaasi, presented me with a seemingly interesting case. Considered Kpaasi's foster mother and Kpaasi's father's sister, I was perceived as being part of the social field. Bio would consider me, as the sister of his sister's husband, an in-law. And, finally, I was asked for help by Djamila herself; therefore she perceived me as a member of the kin group as well as a white person who might have further resources to help her. All these factors gave me a social role in the field and, even more specifically, the kinship roles of being Kpaasi's mother and his father's sister. Therefore I decided not to seek a solution from "outside" but left the conflict to be negotiated within existing kinship ties. The only thing I wanted to make sure of was that Djamila's voice was heard insofar as she would not remain exploited in a miserable situation. Therefore I used my role as a member of the kinship web to discuss the conflict with the relevant members of the family.

I'll now analyze the story by outlining the central role of sibling relations at different stages in Djamila's life. I do so by describing the perspectives of the different actors involved.

Searching for Brotherly Support in Marriage Crises and Other Problems: Amana, Djamila's Mother

Starting with Djamila's mother and her relation to her brother, it is important to know some background about both and, more generally, about the obligations men have toward their sisters. Djamila's mother, Amana, was born in the village of Tɛbɔ. However, she did not spend her childhood in her paternal home but as a foster child in another village, which she left for her first marriage. She was married three times. Her first marriage was childless; during the second one she gave birth to two daughters and Kpaasi. Whereas the girls grew up with foster parents, Kpaasi remained with his biological father when Amana returned to her paternal home and divorced.

Then she married a relatively poor man in Nikki, a nearby small, quite rural town, and gave birth to five children—Djamila the first born. During the time of being married—most Baatombu woman marry various times during the life course—women can always return to their paternal home when problems arise. Amana did so several times when she had trouble with her husbands or financial problems. After the death of their father, brothers have to continue caring for their sisters whenever they need it. Finally, many Baatombu women return to their paternal home after their menopause; then too the brothers have the obligation to provide them with food and care. It is this relatedness that made Amana consider her paternal home in Tɛbɔ as her real home where she went when she needed help or support.

In her particular case, the role of having to care for his adult sister's problems is mainly fulfilled by Bio. For, among the several siblings of Amana, Bio is the only one who attended school and gained economic wealth. Therefore he is the only brother on whom Amana can count in a crisis.

Taking Responsibility for Younger Brother and Sister's Child: Bio

Having been the secretary of the village cooperative in Tɛbɔ for a while, Bio has fulfilled an important social role in the village. As one of the richest farmers in the village, he later became a professional in the regional peasant cooperative. He is married to Alima, an urban-born wife with whom he lives in middle-class fashion in Nikki. Nevertheless, he regularly comes to Tɛbɔ to look after his fields.

Bio played an important role for his sister Amana not only by intervening in moments of crisis and providing a home in Tɛbɔ but also by fostering her daughter, Djamila's younger sister, whom he sent to school and raised in his household in Nikki. He also took responsibility for other relatives, among them his younger brother David, who finished secondary school and is now attending university. This can be understood as being one of the new foster arrangements previously mentioned in which successful urban adults foster their rural younger siblings in order to help them in their own lives and careers. But because Bio also took Amana's daughter in to live with him, he expressed responsibility not only for his own siblings but also for the children of his sister. The relationship between Bio and Amana could therefore be seen as an example of a solid relation fulfilling the role expectations between an adult married woman and her brother. It is quite typical that this sibling relation was of no importance when both were children, since Amana and Bio did not grow up together, but developed when they were grown adults with children of their own. Therefore the relation between them can be seen as an example of how sibling relations change over the different phases of the life course. By fostering one of her children and hosting her in situations of crises, Bio had fulfilled Amana's role expectations, which made it difficult for her to oppose him when he ordered that Djamila live with his in-laws in Cotonou.

Being Sister and Wife: Alima, Bio's Wife

The position of Bio is determined by his being not only Amana's brother but also the husband of Alima, a woman with an urban background. She is close to her sister, a woman who lives, together with her husband, in an urban, middle-class household in Cotonou. Both were well educated and obtained attractive jobs in the formal sector.

This sister, Amouzatou, asked Alima to look for a rural girl in order to help her with her newborn son, so that she could continue her professional career. Normally, it is very unusual for Baatombu to give their children into the households of in-laws, as Bio did. I'll later give some reasons for why he did, but regardless, with this act he did something for his wife's kin and, thus, for his acceptance as her husband and their in-law. Therefore, once it had taken place, it would create marital problems for Bio to take Djamila out of the household of his wife's sister. This was a key argument he often repeated when explaining his inaction to me. Looking at the role of Bio leads me, thus, to understand that having to perform different kinship roles at the same time, such as being a husband and a brother, creates conflicts. The same could be argued in the case of his wife: giving a working girl to her sister meant that Alima performed well as a sister, but this act also created the potential for a conflict with her husband and his family.

Growing Up with Parents' Siblings and Sharing Everyday Life with Foster Siblings: Djamila's Childhood

Djamila is the main figure in the conflict. Since her early childhood, her life course was strongly shaped by different siblings of her parents. Therefore this phase in her life could be seen as an excellent example of the intergenerational dimensions of siblingship and, moreover, the power adults have over the children of their siblings. Djamila's childhood could also be understood as an example of the pitfalls of a special kind of sibling relation that results from the foster arrangement with parents' siblings: relations with step- or foster brothers and sisters.

Djamila grew up with her biological parents until she was five years old. She attended kindergarten and was ready to enter primary school when her paternal aunt came and asked for her as a foster girl. Although the mother was against it,[9] she was unable to resist because accordingly to Baatombu norms, a father's sister has the right to take the first-born child of her brother. As a result, Djamila did not go to school but went to the household of her paternal aunt where she helped her father's sister sell food in the market in Nikki. But from the beginning, there were many conflicts. Like many children who grew up as foster children, she felt that she did not have the same position in the household as the biological children of her foster mother. Not only were the biological children sent to school, while she had to work in the market; she was also not cared for in the same way as the biological children of her foster mother. Djamila told me that whenever money was missing, she was accused of having stolen it, especially by her social sisters and brothers. This happened although she once saw her foster brother entering the mother's room, where the money was hidden, and taking some of it. She was beaten regularly and did not get the same food as did her siblings. Therefore Djamila did not grow up feeling close to her social brothers and sisters. Rather, the adults differentiated between them and, as a consequence, conflicts and accusations among the siblings dominated her childhood.

From time to time she went to her mother, who also lived in Nikki, and complained about her situation. But the mother always answered that she could not take her away since Djamila was fostered by the paternal sister of her father, as was expected for a married couple's first child.

After Djamila had run away several times from her aunt, her father finally agreed that she could leave the place. Nevertheless, since it is shameful among the Baatombu to reclaim one's own child, her parents did not want to take her back. In order to avoid a conflict with his sister, Djamila's father preferred that his daughter live with her married cousin in a nearby village. At that time, she was about thirteen years old and considered a youngster nearly ready to marry, rather than a child. She felt relatively comfortable with her cousin, but after several months she was told that Bio, her maternal uncle, had decided to send her to Cotonou, to the household of his wife's sister. Again, a sibling of her parents had intervened.

Dowry and Morality: Negotiating Djamila's Youth without Her Involvement

One of the conflicts that had created the tensions with her aunt and first foster mother was the question of schooling and apprenticeship. Djamila told me that her aunt always promised to pay for her marriage and dowry, while she wanted to go to school, and, when this was no longer possible, at least to learn a trade. In recent years, it has become obligatory for Baatombu foster parents to fund either a dowry or an apprenticeship for their foster girls. This is one reason the social and economic costs make running away from foster parents a difficult choice for a girl. By running away, a girl risks losing her dowry or apprenticeship and, therefore, a very important investment in her future. Accordingly, after running away, Djamila's situation became difficult. First, the relation between her father and his sister deteriorated. Second, she was now at an age when marriage or apprenticeship should have been the next step, but there was nobody willing to pay for this, since her biological parents refused on the grounds that they feared someone would accuse them of having taken their daughter away from the foster mother.

Third, there was a common fear, expressed mainly by male relatives, that she might get pregnant and be "spoiled" without a proper marriage or training. As Djamila had already become a teenager, she was seen as a young girl at risk of pregnancy. Staying in the household and being under the control of somebody "serious" might save her from the danger of losing, through an "immoral way of life," her dowry and chances of a good marriage. As this discourse was much more shared by men—Bio as well as Kpaasi shared these thoughts frequently with me—it could be interpreted as being a justification for her being sent to the in-laws by Bio. However, it also represented male thinking about similar cases like Djamila's. One of the suggestions is, of course, that if anything happens and fails with the career of a girl, it is, in the end, her behavior that provoked it. Djamila herself was not asked for her opinion.

It was at this stage, so Bio told me, that he got an inquiry through his wife that her sister in Cotonou needed a girl to help her in the house and to take care of her newborn child. He immediately agreed to send Djamila to them.

According to earlier norms of fosterage among the Baatombu, only the classificatory parents and the classificatory brothers and sisters of a man or a woman have the right to claim a child (Alber 2004b). The request of Bio's wife's sister was, therefore, against the norms. Normally, children are not given to in-laws, but in Djamila's case it was unclear who would take in this nearly grown-up girl. Because of the tensions between Djamila's father and his sister, who had been her foster mother, she could not stay with her biological parents in Nikki. This is why it looked like a good solution to send Djamila to Cotonou. As her mother's brother, Bio had, in any case, special authority over the girl.

Searching for Rescue from an Unknown Brother: Djamila in Cotonou

Djamila and her parents were told that she would stay in Cotonou for just a few months, in order to help her uncle's in-laws, and that she would have the opportunity to learn French. But since the woman she worked for became pregnant again, she stayed in Cotonou for two and a half years, up to the delivery of the second child. In Cotonou, she was treated like a domestic worker, sleeping on the floor of the living room when the other family members went to bed, locked into the house all day, and having to do the housework while the mother of the family went to work. In fact when one entered the household, Djamila behaved just like other domestic workers, who nowadays frequently work in West African urban households. For example, when I visited the household together with her brother Kpaasi, Djamila served us cold drinks in the living room, but after serving us, despite the fact that we were visiting *her*, she left the room and remained in the kitchen. She was, then, not performing at all like a sister but remained in the role of the invisible and nameless domestic worker. When the housewife or her husband were present, there was never any "structural equivalence of the sibling group" between Djamila and Kpaasi. However, unlike other domestic workers, Djamila was not paid.

Her situation was the outcome of an unusual mix of different norms—that is, "rural" norms, according to which children are placed in households as members of the family, and "urban" norms, which involve sharp differences in clothing, food, and naming between domestic workers and family members. This mixture was very advantageous for the urban family and quite disadvantageous for Djamila. Her treatment complied neither with the rural norms, which prescribe that all children should be treated equally, nor with urban rules that domestic workers, who differ from foster children in their status within the household, receive wages.

This mixture of foster norms with norms regarding the employment of girls was possible only because at that time there was no social control from Djamila's family. None of them lived in (or traveled regularly to) Cotonou and thus no one was able to observe the conditions under which she had to live. Moreover, those who were responsible for the arrangement, especially Bio, did not behave as if they were attached or committed to the girl.

This lack of social control changed when David, Bio's younger brother for whom he paid university tuition fees, visited the household. He told Djamila that one of her maternal half-brothers was now living in Cotonou. This was Kpaasi, David's nephew, to whom he is close; both are of the same age. They had spent their early childhood in the village of Tɛbɔ together. Afterwards, both went to the city to continue schooling, but, despite being hosted in different households, they remained close and shared the hardships of their respective arrangements. In a way, even though they were formally uncle and nephew, they could be considered "brothers" because of shared joy and suffering over their lifetimes. They say about each other that they are close friends.[10]

Djamila herself did not know Kpaasi very well. They had seen each other briefly from time to time in Nikki, but because he was not the son of her father but a child from a former marriage of her mother, they had never lived together. Up to that day, Kpaasi had been (just as she had been to Kpaasi) one of those relatives of no importance in her life. But, like all kin, he was a potential resource that could be mobilized in special situations, and as a brother, he could be seen as a man who should care for her. David gave her Kpaasi's mobile phone number, which is also a typical behavior among youngsters, and it was an expression of the closeness between David and Kpaasi. Up to that moment, Kpaasi had never entered into the household of his uncle's in-laws, so it was David who gave him access to them by giving his relatives Kpaasi's telephone number.

When she got it, Djamila immediately called her then almost-unknown brother Kpaasi and gave him her address. Subsequently, Kpaasi visited the household from time to time. On these occasions, she complained about her situation. In the beginning, Kpaasi told me, he did not want to help her. Since she had been sent to Cotonou by a maternal uncle and Kpaasi had never been consulted in the matter, he felt that if he interfered, he would put himself in a difficult situation.

One day, however, Kpaasi casually told me the story from his point of view. I was astonished to learn that Kpaasi had a sister living in Cotonou, and we decided to visit her. We were able to have a long conversation because she was alone with the small children at home.

She explained her situation, and I came to the conclusion that Djamila was being exploited in the house of the in-laws of her uncle. Since I had to leave the country the following day, Kpaasi promised to talk to Bio. He was told that if he was interested in the girl's future, he should take her into his own household. However, Kpaasi was a student who shared a flat with other students and could not afford to take his sister in at his own cost. Therefore he was afraid to enter too deeply into the conflict, since that would mean that he would become responsible for his sister, a prospect he felt he was too young and too poor to take on.

Nevertheless, Kpaasi's conversation with his uncle changed the situation for Djamila. The relatives involved could no longer close their eyes completely to her situation. This created a minimum of kinship-based social control and thereby signaled to the family of the in-laws that Djamila's family knew about the harshness of her situation in Cotonou.

When I came back to Benin several months later, I also talked to Bio about Djamila. He explained to me that he was in a very complicated situation and justified his behavior with the arguments I had already mentioned: If he had left her in Nikki, she would have become pregnant and immoral. He had put her to the in-laws in Cotonou in order to open a way for a better future by creating an opportunity for her to learn French and become familiar with urban life. If he now took Djamila away from the in-laws in Cotonou, he would cause a conflict with his wife. He told me that it would be impossible for him to take her into his own household.

In the end, my field assistant Bake, a woman from Parakou, intervened in our conversation. She suggested that if Bio agreed to pay for an apprenticeship for Djamila in Parakou, she would look for a tailor's workshop to accept the girl. To my surprise, Bio agreed, if Bake promised to arrange this.

Some months later, when I visited Benin again, I met Djamila in Bake's household in Parakou. After Bio had finally agreed to pay for the apprenticeship, Bake and her husband had offered Djamila a place in their own household. In order to avoid any conflict with his own siblings and those of his wife, Bio dared ask neither his in-laws nor Djamila's parents to pay for her training. Since he had once taken in Djamila and given her to his in-laws, her parents considered him the person responsible for her well-being, which included payments for whatever was necessary in order for her to become an adult.

Becoming a Brother: Kpaasi

Despite the fact that she has never been asked about what she wanted or asked to take the initiative, Djamila herself took the initiative to change her situation and influence how and with whom she had to live several times. In Nikki, when she was unhappy with having to live with her father's sister and some social siblings whom she could not trust, she ran away. As she went to her biological parents, the place she went to in search of rescue was also kinship based.

The same could be said about her agency in order to change her unhappy place in Cotonou with the in-laws of her mother's brother. In Cotonou, she looked for contact, first to David, the younger brother of Bio, who had brought her into the situation she was in. Second, she called her brother Kpaasi. She expected help because he was her brother. As a student who also lived in Cotonou, he seemed to be able to fulfill the role expectation that adult brothers should help their sisters when they get into trouble. But Kpaasi did not respond immediately. At first, he tried to avoid the contact with his sister, whom he did not know well and for whom he did not want to take responsibility. "I was not asked when she was sent to Cotonou; nobody asked my point of view," he once told me. "It is those who decided who should now find a solution to the problem."

For some time, he tried to avoid acting as a brother, by not visiting Djamila regularly and continuing to live his own life in Cotonou far from her. This was possible since he had never lived with her before. But Djamila always addressed him as her brother, up to the point that he started to behave as such. After Djamila had called him several times and it became clear that he could no longer ignore the issue, he spoke to me. Only when I agreed to get involved by visiting his sister did he become more engaged in the conflict. Later on, Kpaasi was perceived as being Djamila's brother by other persons also, which implied even more that he had to care for her. This happened, for instance, when I got interested in Djamila's life and asked Kpaasi to accompany me to visit her in Cotonou. But it was also the case during the time Djamila was living in the household of Bake.

As I already mentioned, Djamila was brought into the household of my field assistant, Bake, who kindly accepted her in her house and managed to find an apprenticeship for her. Bake had convinced Bio that he had to pay for the apprenticeship. But as he had, at the beginning, paid only half of the sum, Bake sent Kpaasi several times to Bio, his mother's brother, in order to make him pay the rest.

When, about one year later, Djamila had become pregnant and her HIV infection was diagnosed, Bake immediately took the decision to throw her out. Again, she called Kpaasi and asked him to accompany his sister back to her parents. And again, Kpaasi was forced to behave as a brother; he travelled with her and brought her and the baby back to her biological parents.[11]

His being made a brother by others could also be observed regarding Bio's wife's sister. Some months after Djamila had left her household, I had the chance to speak directly with her. At that moment, Amouzatou accused Kpaasi of having caused the whole conflict. According to her, it had been his intervention and his wrong ideas about the exploitation of his sister that had made Djamila question her situation in Cotonou and in their household. "If her brother had not made contact with his sister and troubled her mind," Amouzatou argued, "she would have remained peacefully in Cotonou." Again, Kpaasi was made a brother by the behavior of others who placed him in a central position in the conflict. The accusation was in fact that by performing too much as a brother, his way of protecting her gave her the wrong ideas.

Of course, Amouzatou's discourse could be understood as an act of justifying her behavior and, indirectly, blaming me, since Djamila expressed frequently that she did not feel happy in the household. Amouzatou's argument was that the appearance of kin, and more precisely a brother, had caused the conflict, because he gave Djamila the wrong ideas by agitating against the family of the in-laws of his uncle. Less negatively, her argument confirmed the importance of kin relations as a means of social control. Without the social control by her brother, Djamila would, probably, still be with the family of her mother's brother's in-laws in Cotonou. In fact, what Amouzatou regretted was that via modern communication technologies and an increasing mobility, even in Cotonou, five hundred kilometers away from the rural home of a girl and in a completely different social setting, there could be some social control through the presence of members of the kin group—specifically a brother. If it was kinship ties—the power of a respected mother's brother and his duties to his in-laws—that brought Djamila into her miserable situation, it was in the end the potential of mobilizing kinship—a brother—that helped her to escape.

Kpaasi himself was fully aware of the strong pressures of kinship obligations. His fear was not only that he might provoke a serious family conflict but also that he would be forced to take Djamila to live with him, which he would not have been able to afford. But it also became very clear that Kpaasi's role in the conflict was, somewhat unexpectedly for Bio's urban in-laws, to provide the necessary social control.

CONCLUSIONS

Sibling relations are at the heart of kinship relations, as the case study has shown. It is not only marriage relations or parenting that constitutes kinship but the relations between siblings and their intergenerational dynamics. The density and the dynamics of kinship relations that change over time became obvious in Djamila's story only by focusing on the many sibling relations. A perspective on marriage would have reduced the story to troubles between in-laws; a perspective on descent to her growing up as a foster child. All these themes are present; however, they do not explain the complexity of the story. This is only possible if one takes the long-lasting and changing sibling relations into account: those between Djamila and Kpaasi, between Bio and Amana, between Djamila and her father's sister, and between Bio's wife and her sister Amouzatou, to mention only those of major relevance.

These sibling relations contribute to the construction of a dense web of inter- and intragenerational kinship relations underestimated in kinship studies. It is the sisters and brothers of the parents, not the parents themselves, who act on and decide the future of a girl. What makes the web especially dense is the fact that sibling relations provide an important social resource throughout the life course. Djamila did not discover Kpaasi during childhood but at a later stage in her life. Bio became important for Amana when she was already married. Sibling relations can gain in importance, while others may lose their significance in everyday life. The relation between Alima and her sister in Cotonou is another vivid example of how sibling relations gain in importance in different phases of the life course, as

Amouzatou needed help during her pregnancies. They had access to different resources through their rural and urban connections, which they relied on one another to provide.

There is a strong expectation of support and help among Baatombu siblings. Kpaasi could hardly refuse Djamila's demands outright, as Bio's wife could hardly resist sending somebody to her sister in town or, at least, showing the will to do so. Analyzing Kpaasi's behavior, it also becomes clear that brother- and sisterhood cannot be understand exclusively as a *given* kinship relation but one that is *made* by the social behavior of the siblings themselves as well as of other related people. By calling Kpaasi, Djamila made him her brother. Later on, others like Bake, Amouzatou, and I confirmed this by addressing him as her brother and expecting brotherly behavior from him. Like other kinship relations, siblingship has a social dimension that confirms, contradicts, interprets, or transforms the biological one. And it can be denied, as Kpaasi tried to do so at first.

In the story of Djamila, brother- and sisterhood in these intergenerational relations means the existence of both strong social control and social pressure, which I tried to express with the metaphoric image of a *thicket* instead of Fortes's metaphor of the *web* of kinship. People are afraid to act against the will of their brothers and sisters, because they fear to be publicly humiliated by them. Moreover, they fear to break the norms of fosterage, because this would make people gossip about them. There is a precarious balance between the social control that causes the norms of good behavior toward foster children to be respected, on the one hand, and other kinds of behavior that do not respect these norms, on the other.

Additionally, I see another balance regarding brother- and sisterhood. People are constantly observed by their sisters and brothers, and they do not want to create a conflict with them. This creates the social pressure to accept the right of brothers and sisters over one's own children. Djamila's mother Amana, for instance, did everything possible to avoid blaming her husband's sister (Djamila's first foster mother) for maltreating Djamila, because she feared that she could be blamed for not recognizing her husband's sister's right over the child. So siblings' rights over children create both social pressure that makes people accept their siblings' exploitation of their children through fosterage and a resource in crisis situations. The latter is especially important in the case of married women. All the rural Baatombu women I know try to find a "brother" in the villages where they have married to guarantee social control and security from their family of origin.

At the beginning of my chapter, I argued that, on the one hand, performing as a brother or a sister provides people with rights but also creates obligations and role expectations. On the other hand, experiencing the powerful decisions of siblings (or parent's siblings) could be a harmful experience even as mobilizing sibling relations can help people to get out of difficult situations. The conflict around Djamila has given a vivid example about the density of the transactions that made the web of kinship a real thicket in which she was captured but also offered a window of escape.

Djamila's story also shows that kinship lines of mutual exchange and support cannot be enlarged arbitrarily. They are restricted to those people who, voluntarily or through social norms and social control, respect the rights and duties kinship relations require. The brief lover of Djamila, as well as the relatives of her mother's brother's wife, were outside the reciprocity of these rights and duties. They were part of the thicket Djamila was in, but they did not provide ways for her to escape. Consequently, one frequent comment on the conflict, when I discussed it with Baatombu people not involved, was that one should never give a girl to one's in-laws, since they would never care for her as if she was their own sister or daughter.

Djamila's story proves that among the Baatombu the importance of siblingship can hardly be understood without considering child foster practices. And, vice versa, in order to understand foster practices one has to look at siblingship: all the foster relations Djamila had been in, whether with the father's sister or the mother's brother, or even the mother's brother's wife's sister, were based on sibling relations. It is the norms of fosterage that give people power over their siblings' children but also create obligations toward them. These sibling relations and the related foster practices are, in recent times, maintained even if remarkable class differences lead to very different economic situations in which siblings live (see also Coe and Pauli, this volume). This is also a point in the relation between Kpaasi and his sister Djamila. Studying at the university, he started to have access to a better social position than his brothers and sisters. Nevertheless, he keeps close to his rural siblings like Djamila.

In the anthropological literature on Africa, one major argument concerning siblingship, made in the "classic" time of structural functionalism, was Alfred Radcliffe-Brown's concept of the "equivalence of siblings" (1971: 89, see also the introduction of this volume). This argument was linked to his perception of the principle of the "unity of the sibling group" (Radcliffe-Brown 1924 and 1950), defined as a "body of brothers and sisters of a common parentage" having thus not only the same position in the kinship web but also similar interests. In view of the rising social and economic differences between siblings, due to migration and urbanization processes, the concept of the *equivalence of siblings*, if ever having described a social reality adequately, is challenged by the new ways of interaction between siblings. The case of Djamila also proves that new ways of giving and taking siblings have led to new tensions between urban and rural brothers and sisters that would also challenge the idea of the *equivalence of siblings*. And finally, this concept is strongly challenged by inter- or intrafamiliar conflicts as well as by taking fostering into account.

A second point in the anthropological discussion on kinship in Africa concerned the idea that the mother's brother plays a special role for children (Clark 1999, Fortes 1949, Goody 1969: 39–90, Piot 1996, Radcliffe-Brown and Forde 1950). I do not want to go into detail here about the discussions around the mother's brother in Africa, but I stress that they explained very well the importance and particular rights and duties of men concerning the children of their sisters. Barbara Meier (1999) has already argued in relation to that literature that it is not only men who have special rights over their sisters' children but also women who have decision-making power over their siblings' children. Quite often they have the right to take the children of their sisters in order to foster them. In this way, Meier argues, women have special power within their kin group by acting on and influencing the lives of their siblings' children. The story of Djamila confirms Meier's point. Not only her mother's brother, Bio, took her and decided her destiny. When she was young, it was also her father's sister who took her into her household.

Adding to Meier's point, I argue that it is not only the multitude of kinship roles that people perform simultaneously that one has to keep in mind in order to understand their behavior in particular conflicts but also the entanglement of these roles. In the story of Djamila, there is a high degree of ambivalence people have about their siblings' interactions with their sons and daughters. On the one hand, Amana as Djamila's mother expected support from her brother by engaging in the education and promotion of her children. On the other hand, she did not feel able to prohibit his taking Djamila in order to put her into the family of his in-laws. Thus the story vividly explains that Baatombu parents have difficulties defending the interests of their children against powerful siblings. As parents, they fear to intervene, because siblings in general are seen as having the rights to decide the destiny of their nieces and nephews.

There is another conclusion to draw. If the new kinship studies have added to the classical structural-functionalist approaches that the everyday behavior and agency of the actors should not be underestimated, this has led to the assumption that rupture and conflict are at the heart of kinship as well as mutuality, exchange, and the underlying cohesive structure. Obviously, my examination of sibling relations seems, at first glance, to confirm these assumptions, since Djamila's story is a story about conflict and rupture. However, it seems to me that above and beyond the important insights of new kinship studies, and the assumption of the constructivist character of kinship, there is, again, a *new* necessity to explain that kinship relations contribute to social cohesion and mutual obligations that endure across life phases and constitute a foundation on which all the negotiations, conflicts, and interactions build. If rules can only be (re)negotiated or broken if their power is fundamentally accepted, then one has to first explain their power and potential for cohesion. When talking about the thicket of kinship relations in general and the centrality of sibling relations in particular in making them so dense, I have tried to give insight into how sibling relations contribute to the validity of cohesion through kinship (see also the introduction to this volume).

For a better understanding of kinship relations, it is important to look carefully not only at the relations between brothers and sisters but also at their connectedness with other relations. In this chapter, I analyzed the dense interconnections between siblinghood and parenting, especially through the fostering of children. Additionally, I mentioned various connections and entanglements between marriage and siblingship, since it is the task of brothers to protect their sisters in unhappy marriages. Last, but not least, the story of Djamila was meant to illustrate how sibling relations, their meanings, and the concrete ways of performing or denying the role of a brother or sister are changing not only constantly but also under the pressure of changing economic conditions. However, it seems that change does not necessarily mean that their importance will decrease. To the contrary, my impression is that especially in the relations between rural and urban households in northern Benin, relations between siblings are maintaining their significance and are thus a key to understanding how kinship produces cohesion and conflict at the same time.

ACKNOWLEDGMENTS

My chapter is a product of ongoing research in northern Benin that began in 1992. Thanks to my friends, relatives, and interview partners in northern Benin, especially to Djamila and her maternal and paternal relatives. A part of the research was realized in the frame of the research project "Fosterage in Northern Benin," financed by the German research fund. This version was written during my fellowship in the international research center "Work and Human Lifecycle in Global History," which I thank for the space of inspiring academic work without the pressure of time. The discussions in the center made me aware of the significance of the life course for all analysis of kinship and social relatedness. Thanks to Jeannett Martin, Tabea Häberlein, and the coeditors of this volume for their comments on earlier versions of this chapter. Special thanks to Sjaak van der Geest, who encouraged me to keep the theme of siblingship in mind.

CHAPTER 5

WHEN SIBLINGS
DETERMINE YOUR "FATE"
SIBLING SUPPORT AND EDUCATIONAL
MOBILITY IN RURAL NORTHWEST CHINA

Helena Obendiek

Despite more than three decades of a family-planning policy that promotes "one-child only," the majority of China's population still does experience siblingship. People from the age cohorts born during the fertility-friendly Maoist years have, on average, as many as four or five siblings.[1] Among the younger generations born under the strict family-planning policy since the early 1980s, those with rural household registration[2]—slightly more than half of the population—still usually experience siblingship, albeit in much smaller sibling sets than their parents.[3]

I discovered the significance of siblingship for the rural population during research about educational aspirations in Huining, an economically deprived county on the arid loess plateau in China's northwest. In this region, pursuing higher education turned out to be a central social support strategy. Educational credentials, so it was hoped, were to facilitate the permanent rural-to-urban mobility of at least one family member, thus enhancing familial access to valuable urban resources unattainable in the rural locality. In this context, siblingship proved to be a central axis of support in terms of both facilitating education and sharing in its "returns."

In this chapter, I show how state policies in the fields of education, the labor market, and population control intertwine with local understandings of sibling relatedness. Changing policies during three decades in post-Maoist China altered opportunities as well as obligations related to siblingship, thus deeply affecting local practices of sibling relatedness. Specifically, the decisive policy changes of the late 1990s, when China turned from a state-regulated labor market for graduates to an increasingly market-oriented economy, generated two distinct generations in post-Maoist rural China, whose experiences of siblingship, mediated by schooling, differed decisively.

Rapid economic development as well as the fast spread of consumer culture spurred by China's increasing market orientation has been blamed for disrupting moral relationships in the countryside (Liu 2000), bringing about a rise of egotism and the "uncivil individual" among China's rural youth (Yan 2003, 2005, 2009). Contrary to such a diagnosis, I found sibling relationships, although not entirely free from conflict and rivalry, were valued as an important source of security and support in the Chinese countryside. Thomas Hauschild (2008: 205–22) proposes the term *reserve* for those aspects of the local community that persons or groups can use against the destructive forces of the market and that they can draw on and revert to in times of crisis. Reserves may include physical space and tacit local knowledge as well as relationships that are sustained through exchanges, moral obligations, and feelings of closeness. Different from the widespread reductionist view of siblingship as a mere side effect of a central parent-child bond, expressed for example in the "resource dilution" hypothesis of additional children minimizing the family resources available to each child (Blake 1989; Steelman and Powell 1989; Steelman, Werum, and Carter 2002), conditions in my field site instead highlighted the importance of intragenerational sibling relationships in their own right. Far from being merely competitors for familial resources, siblings proved to be important sources of mutual support. This was manifest not only in adult siblings' shared responsibility of providing elder care for their common parents but also in many forms of intragenerational support between siblings from their early childhoods onwards. In view of the continuous lack of social welfare schemes for the rural population, on the one hand, and market reforms in the educational and labor sector since the 1990s, on the other, sibling support seemed to have become increasingly central to local people's everyday lives, so that the interdependence of siblings' "fates" tightened.

In the following sections, I describe how graduates of the early reform-socialist[4] period (1979–97; hereafter named "early graduates") became the "backbones of support" for their siblings who remained in rural Huining as "peasants." I then turn toward the experiences of relatedness between current students or recent graduates and their siblings. I show how in the smaller sibling sets of the later generation,[5] the kind of support for the elderly parents expected from each sibling was determined not only by gender but to a great extent also by educational achievement. At the same time, the rising costs of higher education made sibling support decisive for the realization of individual educational mobility.[6]

How Early Graduates Became the "Backbones of Support"

When China dismissed the radical policies of the Cultural Revolution (1966–76) immediately after Mao's death, the country's return to "normality" became marked by the reintroduction of a merit-based educational system. In the following two decades, a small proportion of rural youth benefitted substantially from their higher education: in the planned economy, advanced educational credentials guaranteed a state-financed pathway into a professional career on the government payroll. For the rural population, education thus became the main road of socioeconomic mobility. State allocation of work in the urban sector was experienced as a "change of fate" by rural families, since it meant that at least one family member crossed the rural-urban citizen divide and achieved long-term urban residency and the manifold welfare benefits that went along with it.[7]

Visitors to Huining County can expect to hear numerous stories about successful graduates who have left the region and pursued a state-guaranteed professional career in government institutions or academia since the reinauguration of the national college entrance exam in 1977. The official slogan of "escape poverty through education" (以教育脱贫; *yi jiaoyu tuopin*) is widely cited locally. The slogan is also often exemplified to visitors by villagers who point out empty houses that have been left behind by those whose children's educational success has spurred the whole family's permanent out-migration.

The case of the Zhao family, my host family during my research in a village in rural Huining County, is illustrative of the local saying that "one university student in the family changes the appearance of the whole family" (家出了一个大学生，全家的面貌就变了; *jia chule yige daxuesheng, quan jia de mianmao jiu bianle*). The Zhao family history illustrates that sharing the returns on education is not only a matter of filial reciprocation to one's parents; it is also often targeted at—directly or indirectly—supporting siblings of both genders.

The Zhao Family

In my first conversation with Zhao Mei, a student from rural Huining County studying at Lanzhou University, I had learned about the central role her "fourth (paternal) uncle" played in her family.[8] I thus was not astonished to hear that when I asked Zhao Mei whether her family would host me for a prolonged time of field research, it was her "fourth uncle" who decided the issue, even though he lived in a city in neighboring Qinghai Province, more than two hundred kilometers away from the Zhao family courtyard in the village.

Zhao Wen, Zhao Mei's "fourth uncle," was the fourth brother within a sibling set of six brothers and one sister, all born between 1956 and 1970. He had been lucky to have just the right age for attending the local senior high school that opened in the village in 1974 and was closed down again just after the end of the Cultural Revolution. Among the siblings, the fourth brother thus became the only one to make an education-based career outside the village. At the time of my research, he held a higher-level position in the government of Qinghai Province that was accompanied by the privilege of permanent urban residency, while all his siblings remained in the locality as "peasants."

Zhao Wen's only sister had left the family to live with her in-laws, two hours' walking distance from her natal home. The two elder Zhao brothers had officially separated from the family by taking their share of the common family property and giving up any further claims toward the patrimony. Both had built houses for their conjugal families in the village. Even though the other four brothers were still considered to be members of the joint family, the fourth and the little (sixth) brother were living permanently with their conjugal families in neighboring Qinghai Province.

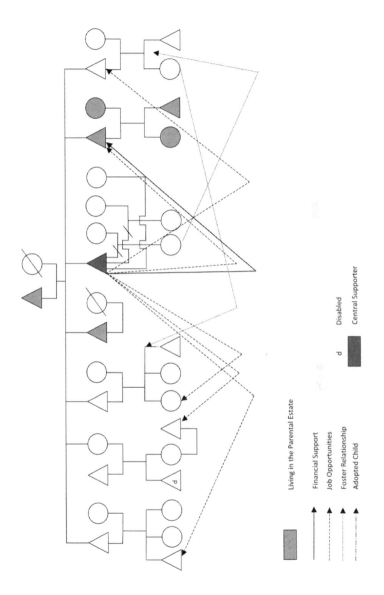

Living in the Parental Estate

Financial Support

Job Opportunities

Foster Relationship

Adopted Child

d   Disabled

Central Supporter

Figure 5.1   The Zhao Family Genealogy

Given the high status the fourth brother, as a government cadre, enjoyed among his siblings, he also acted as the family manager (当家; *dangjia*).[9] Any major event within the family thus first had to be discussed with him, in order to have him decide on further proceedings.

How the Fourth Brother Supported His Siblings

Over the years, the fourth brother had not only contributed to the living expenses of his seventy-three-year-old father with regular monetary gifts. He had also supported each of his six siblings in one way or another. Primarily, he had arranged diverse job opportunities in neighboring Qinghai Province for his siblings. In the case of the older siblings, who were too old to migrate themselves, the fourth brother had helped their sons or sons-in-law with job opportunities. Since the second brother's adopted son was still too young to become a labor migrant, it was the daughter who benefited from the fourth brother's support. He had arranged for her education and later had helped to get her a position as a primary school teacher. The widowed and childless third brother, who was believed to be mentally retarded, had remained in the village to do agricultural work. He was supported by the fourth brother with annual gifts of clothes and small gifts of cash. The fifth brother had benefited from the fourth brother's arrangement of labor migration opportunities, but he had returned to the village when he got a local job that paid better. Since the fifth brother's daughter, Zhao Mei, had proven to be talented in school, the fourth brother contributed substantially to her living expenses and tuition fees. For the little (sixth) brother, the fourth brother had arranged a comparatively well-paid and steady contract job at a state grain distribution station in upland Qinghai Province.

The fourth brother thus had supported all his siblings and/or their offspring. The kind of help arranged for each, however, varied considerably in terms of amount and quality. Moreover, his support had not been unconditional. When the little brother had dropped out of school early, the fourth brother accused him of counting too much on his help instead of managing his future for himself. Settling the quarrel that ensued between the brothers required the intervention of their common father, who was worried about his youngest son's uncertain future.

The Fourth Brother's Support: Not Necessarily a One-Way Street

Obviously, the fourth brother had become the backbone of social support for his natal family. His supportive attitude was praised not only within the Zhao family but also, sometimes with a smack of envy, among the villagers. When taking a closer look, it did, however, become evident that the fourth brother's engagement in supporting his siblings was not entirely unilateral. The position of having the decision-making power in family affairs and being treated as the honored guest with all his rural kin at his beck-and-call during his visits to the village might have been some kind of "symbolic repayment" for the burden of his rural kinship obligations. Yet reciprocity also took more material forms. Since his third wife, a woman with an urban family background, strictly refused to tolerate any contact between her husband and his two daughters from earlier marriages, the fourth brother had to rely on his brothers to fulfill his legal obligations toward his daughters. This included payment of alimonies to his ex-wives and his daughters, who lived near his parental home. The fourth brother sometimes ordered the fifth brother to effect such payments, not always repaying him properly for his expenses, claimed the fifth brother's daughter Zhao Mei. Other monetary transactions with former classmates and friends in rural Huining were also managed by the fourth brother by ordering his brothers to be active on his behalf—for example, in terms of collecting debts. When, in early 2007, expenses for the elderly father's hospital treatment were divided between the brothers, it became obvious that to have arranged a job with a comparatively steady income for his little (sixth) brother was an important relief of the fourth brother's own strained budget, since the little brother thus was not only able but also obliged to contribute substantially to this and other major financial issues that concerned the whole family. Moreover, when his elder daughter faced problems at senior high school in Huining County and a change to a school in Qinghai Province was likely to improve her chances at the national college entrance exam, the fourth brother decided to send her to be fostered in his little (sixth) brother's conjugal family, who also lived in Qinghai Province. To have the daughter live at his own place would not have been an option, given his wife's objections. That his rural siblings were not only a burden but also a reserve for the fourth brother also became evident when he returned to the village to have

Figure 5.2   The Fourth Zhao Brother Toasting His Brothers

the childlessness of his present marriage cured by the ritual specialists at the local shrine. In this and other matters, local spiritual order and his continuous integration in the rural society as an honored person of considerable social standing seemed to be a significant factor in his pursuit of security and mental peace.

When chatting with the fourth brother during one of his visits to the village about his motivation to support all his siblings, he explained the social expectation that accompanied social advancement:

> If you have the (cap)ability (本事; *benshi*), but do not help others, you are not a good person. People will talk badly about you. If you help others, you are a good person in other people's eyes. In China, people evaluate others only according to the power (权利; *quanli*) they hold. If you have the ability to help others, like your family, you prove to be trustworthy and to have integrity (信任; *xinren*). You demonstrate your good character (人品; *renpin*) and that is why people trust you. In the urban context the famous saying that "If you have made your way up, all the chicken and dogs follow and fly high with you" (一人得道,鸡犬升天; *yi ren de dao, ji chou sheng tian*[10]) somehow smacks of nepotism.

But I still think that to help your family members is a Chinese virtue
(美德; *meide*). (field notes, February 19, 2007)

However, later the same day he made clear that his support was not
necessarily motivated by the Chinese virtue of sharing one's success
(see also Yan 1996: 129f) when he whispered to me, "Concerning
your question today why I support them all, I tell you, after my father's
death, I will support none of them any longer." Besides reconfirming
the centrality of the filial bond, this statement also revealed the exhaus-
tion and frustration of being the only member of the family who had
achieved socioeconomic mobility. Like a "patron," the fourth brother
cared for his "clients": his siblings. With no other source of support
available, the latter always turned toward their "successful" brother
for solving the numerous financial problems their poor and insecure
local living conditions entailed.

How Typical Is the Zhao Family?

Compared to other local families, the case of the Zhao family is char-
acteristic in some respects and exceptional in others.[11] Graduates of
the early generation with rural Huining family backgrounds usually
had large sets of six to ten siblings. If formal education had been an
option at all, it had been that for only one or, at most, a few siblings
of a family. Among the siblings, educational opportunities had been
distributed according to various factors, including gender, position in
the sibling set, physical condition, educational capabilities, parental
preferences, and, as in the case of the fourth Zhao brother, the for-
tune of being the right age at a certain historical point in time when
the oscillating (educational) policies happened to be beneficial. Minor
age differences could thus sometimes be blamed for causing highly
divergent educational "fates" between siblings, which later were to
cause tremendous asymmetries in their living conditions.

In general, graduates of the first two post-Maoist decades thus were
either the only sibling or one of a few who had taken the educational
pathway out of the locality, had benefited from the state job-allocation
system, and later were to enjoy a stable working position that provided permanent urban residency, a regular salary, and access to social
welfare, including health insurance and pension schemes. Such "successful" graduates usually had a number of siblings with rural family

registrations who neither had steady income nor were eligible for any kind of social welfare, and thus were in constant need of support when it came to financing their children's education and marriages or covering other major expenses, such as health treatment. Besides the financial support, an educated sibling was usually an important resource also in terms of information and social contacts that could prove helpful in the arrangement of urban job opportunities, educational opportunities, and hospital treatment, for instance.

The return to an economy that recoupled educational success to state-guaranteed permanent rural-to-urban mobility after the Cultural Revolution thus generated a world of difference between the living conditions of the educationally successful and their rural siblings. Having gained access to numerous urban resources, "early graduates" thus were in the position to turn into the "backbone of support" for their siblings who remained in the villages.

Local Notions of Siblingship

Family histories collected in rural Huining County exposed numerous cases of sibling relationships that had been broken off. Nevertheless, people subscribed to the "naturalness" of solidarity and mutual help between siblings. "Natural" sibling solidarity was explained locally by biological arguments of descent, such as relatedness through "blood" (血亲; *xueqin*), "bones and flesh" (亲骨肉; *qin gu rou*), or "same womb" (同胞; *tongbao*). Mutual obligations between adopted or stepsiblings were similarly interpreted as based on shared substance, albeit not a biological one. What was shared were the parents as a source of attention and care.

Irrespective of the level of emotional attachment between siblings, there was a clear moral obligation to support one's siblings in cases of emergency. For the villagers, the norm of sibling support, especially strict for brothers, was backed up by strong social sanctions in the community. Obligations of sibling support even outweighed the tragic consequences they might cause for one's own conjugal family. Such was the case with student Zhu Jinyan's father, whose brother had caused a lethal accident. Only payment of a large compensation sum would save the latter from going to jail. Given the high social pressure of sibling solidarity, Zhu Jinyan's father had little choice but

Figure 5.3   Connected through Shared Substance: Five Sisters

to sacrifice the educational opportunities of his children and provide the money for saving his brother from such a grim fate. "Had my father behaved differently, it would have been his social death in the village," twenty-year-old Zhu Jinyan commented.

In view of such a strong norm of mutual responsibilities between siblings, on the one hand, and the highly vulnerable conditions of everyday life in rural China, on the other, where hardly any welfare schemes protect people against risk, having siblings with access to urban resources can improve villagers' safety nets considerably.

Conditions of Sibling Support

Most graduates of the early reform period explained their feelings of obligation toward their siblings as the result of the support they had received from them in the past. Stories of siblings contributing their labor or income to the family economy or sacrificing their own educational opportunities in favor of the graduate were frequently recalled. Yet, some graduates of the early reform period felt they owed their success solely to their own studiousness and stressed instead how they had supported their families by living frugally and sending home portions of their state-provided student stipends.

The burden of having siblings in the countryside produced varied responses. Some graduates claimed that, as beneficiaries of current rural-urban economic disparities, it was no big deal for them to support their siblings in the village in financial matters, since what was a small sum of money in the urban context meant a lot in the countryside. Other graduates experienced their support obligations toward rural siblings as more burdensome. "We graduates with rural family backgrounds have to support all our family members in the countryside. We therefore just do not dare to spend our money for ourselves and enjoy the pleasures of urban life like the real urbanites do," commented Zhang Jun, a teacher from Huining County who lived in Lanzhou.

The range of support actually provided by graduates for their rural siblings is difficult to assess, since sibling support is given across the life span and might vary considerably over time. In addition, the amount of support given might be interpreted differently by the provider and recipient.

In fact, the general claim of "Of course I support my siblings!" among graduates of the early reform period often reflected normative expectations only or was limited to cases of emergency. In practice, sibling support was hardly unconditional. In more intimate conversations, graduates sometimes admitted that support obligations toward their siblings caused quarrels between them and their marital partners. This was especially the case in "rural-urban" marriages, when familial support obligations were considered to be unevenly distributed between the partners. In "rural-rural" marriages, female graduates often complained about the asymmetry of the support drawn from the marital budget in favor of their in-laws in comparison to their natal kin. While supporting parents usually was reported to be only a minor matter of debate between the spouses, because it was based on the norm of filial piety, support of siblings and their conjugal families often stirred up greater marital disagreements.

On the other hand, graduates often considered the financial demands of their rural siblings toward them to be unrealistically high, with siblings almost willingly exaggerating the graduates' actual financial capabilities. Requests for financial support were usually negotiated so that in the end a reduced amount of money was given, since "to give nothing is impossible." Before giving great sums of money, graduates preferred sustainable ways of help, such as providing the sibling with income-earning opportunities through financing a start-up of a small local business or, most favored, by supporting the siblings' children.

The employment opportunities graduates arranged for siblings in the city usually meant hard physical labor under insecure working conditions. Moreover, such employment was only a short- or medium-term solution, since rural migrants would be forced to return to the countryside once the marketability of their physical labor deteriorated. Supporting education was, however, believed to facilitate long-term rural-to-urban mobility and access to mental instead of manual labor. In addition, graduates faced a particular moral pressure to pass on their cultural capital to other family members. Since their siblings usually were too old to continue their schooling themselves, graduates often accomplished support for their siblings indirectly by supporting the education of their siblings' offspring. Given the customary ethic of filial piety as well as children's jural obligation to provide elderly care for their parents, it was taken for granted that improved living conditions of nieces and nephews "naturally" would benefit their parent, the sibling of the supportive graduate.[12] Educational support provided by graduates toward their nieces and nephews was thus locally interpreted as indirect horizontal sibling support, effected diagonally[13] via the next generation. Accordingly, graduate Song Zhuomei summarized, "Supporting my brother's children means supporting him."

While the policies of the first two post-Maoist decades caused great discrepancies in the living conditions of the "early graduates" and their rural siblings, reforms in the educational and labor market sector of the late 1990s dramatically changed the costs and effects of higher education. The next generation of students and graduates thus faced rather different conditions of sibling relatedness.

CURRENT STUDENTS, RECENT GRADUATES, AND THEIR SIBLINGS

Current students and recent graduates who took the national college entrance exam in the late 1990s grew up with firsthand impressions of their predecessors, the "backbones of support," who were held in high esteem locally. As role models, if not as actual supporters,

graduates of the early reform period had helped to foster local children's educational motivation. However, for the latter, conditions
of study as well as employment prospects were rather different from
what their predecessors had enjoyed.

In the late 1990s, a new wave of market reforms turned higher
education into an increasingly expensive "private" endeavor. At the
same time, the state gradually retreated from providing jobs for the
graduates. Tuition and fees rose spectacularly, so they came to cover as
much as a third of the total funds spent on higher education in 2008
(Dong and Wan 2012: 2). It was no coincidence that the introduction
of a "users' pay" system in China's higher-education sector occurred
precisely when the first generation of children born under the family-
planning policy came of age. In fact, the assumption that parents of
only one child were willing to invest more in that child played an
important role in the policy change (Bai 2006, Kipnis 2009). From
the beginning, the international experience of rising child-rearing
costs causing reduced fertility rates as well as increased parental investment in child rearing had led Chinese demographers to aim at the
same results by way of "reverse social engineering" (Kipnis 2009).
Reduced fertility was expected to induce increasing parental investment, thus enhancing the overall "quality" of the children.[14]

At the same time the educational sector expanded rapidly, with enroll-
ment rates in institutions of higher education quadrupling between
1998 and 2004 (Bai 2006: 130f). While the percentage of rural youth
attaining higher education rose considerably, these students had to
depend heavily on their families' willingness and ability to support
their educational endeavor. Moreover, the state retreated from its former responsibility of assigning an urban job to every graduate, so that
increasing numbers of graduates faced difficulties in entering satu-
rated markets for qualified labor.

Reforms in the educational sector meant that, unlike the early graduates whose state stipends often had been high enough to allow them
to skim some money off to support their families, the later generation
of students depended heavily on familial financial support, while the
returns on such educational investment in terms of later employment
became increasingly insecure.

With family budgets constrained, having siblings—the case for most
current students and recent graduates from my field site[15]—could be

Figure 5.4   Preparing for the National College Entrance Exam in Huining County

a burden as well as an asset. Within local sibling sets of usually two to four children, each sibling competed for a share of the strained family budget. Yet, because rural Huining parents' incomes usually were insufficient to support the higher education of even a single child, educational opportunities became more dependent on sibling support. More often than not, the support from a sibling working in the city or doing other temporary jobs was crucial for financing further education. Older siblings who themselves attended or had attended institutions of higher education might, moreover, provide crucial support for their younger sibling's education other than in purely financial ways. In any case, support among siblings entailed an explicit obligation of reciprocity at a later point in time when the former supporter would be in need. This was all the more so since high educational spending, coupled with the recently insecure returns on educational investment, put whole families into severe financial difficulties. At the same time, without an elderly pension system for the rural population, siblings continued to share a common, albeit gendered, responsibility for the well-being of elderly parents. Consequently, conditions of the later reform-socialist period caused students' and their siblings' "fates" to become closely intertwined in intergenerational as well as in intragenerational terms.

In the next section, I first highlight how, for current students and recent graduates, education affects the (gendered) intergenerational obligations siblings share toward their parents. I then show that, for this generation, sibling support in the field of education may also be interpreted as an intragenerational investment into the supporter's own future social security, even though the outcome of such investment has become increasingly insecure.

Education and (Gendered) Intergenerational Support Obligations

Despite national legislation that defines intergenerational obligations toward parents as equally shared among the children of both genders, in rural Huining County, local perceptions were clearly shaped by the customary patrilineal notion of daughters leaving their natal family on marriage, while sons (and their wives respectively) would take over the role of caregivers of elderly parents. Customarily, the duty of caring for the elderly parents was assigned to the youngest among the sons, who in turn inherited the family estate. Nowadays it is rather the level of education that determines who will fill this role.

A case in point was twenty-six-year-old recent graduate Fang Yubo from rural Huining, with whose family in the village I stayed for some days. Fang Yubo's situation demonstrates the complex burden many recent graduates from rural Huining face.

Fang Yubo had graduated from university in 2004 and had been lucky to find employment in a government department in Lanzhou, where his brother, older than him by one year, worked as a labor migrant. During their childhoods, the financial situation of the family had been too tight to pay the costs of both sons' education. Fate between the brothers was sealed when Fang Yubo's older brother failed the secondary high school entrance exam twice, while Fang Yubo passed the exam in his second attempt. The older brother then left the village as a labor migrant. After a couple of years, he brought back home his newly wed wife, who remained in the village with her in-laws. From his earnings the older brother remitted money home to support his parents, to contribute to Fang Yubo's daily living expenses at university, and to pay the expenses of their little sister, who attended secondary high school.

From the day Fang Yubo graduated from university, the flows of support in the family changed drastically. The older brother stopped all payments toward his parents, his younger brother, and his sister. Since the parents earned no cash income from their agricultural labor, Fang Yubo became responsible for paying his parents' annual expenses of 1,500 yuan for coal and fertilizer. He also had to provide his younger sister's tuition and living expenses of about 9,000 yuan annually, for which he had to take out a high-interest loan. Besides these familial support obligations, he still had to pay back his own student loan of 24,000 yuan. Since graduation, Fang Yubo had thus been borrowing from friends and juggling bank loans. He was, of course, comparatively lucky to be in a steady position with a monthly salary of 1,400 yuan. In order to save as much of his income as possible, he lived in the triple-bed dormitory provided by his company. However, how to deal with his familial obligations and still manage marriage to his girlfriend, which entailed buying an apartment in the city, was a mystery to him.

Fang Yubo's case shows how education impacts brothers' support obligations toward their parents. Since in rural Huining County inheritance of the parental house was no longer considered to be a significant economic asset, it was rather the level of education that eventually determined the different roles brothers were to take in familial support. School dropouts had to take on the role of the financial supporter of the family as long as their brothers were still in school. After the latter's graduation, financial obligations shifted to rest on the graduates' shoulders. Correspondingly, since labor migrants were expected to return to the village sooner or later, they (and their wives respectively) would assume the duty of the elderly parents' daily care by co-residence or by living in proximity, while the graduate was expected to provide financial support.

However, in exceptional cases, labor migrants would not return to the countryside but remain outside the village on a long-term basis. According to Fang Yubo, this goal was what his older brother saved all his money for after he had stopped all payments to his natal family. Only in rare instances did migrant brothers of male graduates separate officially from the parental household and leave both kinds of burden, financial support as well as the day-to-day care for the elderly, to their graduate brothers.

Sisters' role in educational support differed from that of brothers. A considerable number of informants recalled that in times of financial shortage it was the sisters who dropped out of school in order to facilitate their brothers' education.[16] Accordingly, if sisters migrated for labor, their remittances home were often used to help finance their brothers' education. Such sisterly support for a brother's education was locally explained as daughters' repayment of the debt accumulated toward the parents for their upbringing, invested indirectly in the betterment of the parents' future living conditions. After all, according to local perception, it was the brother's future that determined the support parents would receive in old age. A sister's financial contribution to her brother's education did not necessarily terminate with her "leaving the family" on marriage. The financial burden of her brother's education might be reckoned in the arrangement of a sister's marriage, since it was seen to affect the future marital budget. In case the groom had a regular income, he might well be expected to contribute substantially.

Besides gender, sibling birth order also shaped support obligations among siblings. When familial resources had been spent on older siblings' education, these students and graduates felt the quasiparental obligation to support their younger siblings' education. Being aware that younger siblings were dependent on them, students who were older siblings often felt forced to compromise their educational opportunities, thus sacrificing their own future life chances. Such missed opportunities included resigning from repetition of the third year of senior high school in order to improve the outcome of the national college entrance exam or refraining from postgraduate studies. Student Meng Wenhong summarized his situation accordingly: "Who would pay for my brother's education if I went for master's studies?"

Yet, for male students, supporting a younger brother's education may also be motivated by an additional aspect. Such was explained to me by student Wang Baoquan.

> *HO:* Do you give him [the younger brother] money when he wants it?
> *Wang Baoquan:* Usually I do, but I give him less, only about half of the amount he asks for . . . I also tutor him. If we both go to university, we can later share the responsibility to support our parents. But if

he does not manage to attend university, and has to stay in the village, I will have to return there often in the future and I will have to give him money, or other material help.

Besides being motivated by the shared intergenerational obligation toward the parents, Wang Baoquan's support for his brother thus also entailed a distinct consideration of his future intragenerational support obligations toward him.

Intragenerational Aspects of Sibling Support

When, in the late 1990s, costs for higher education rose dramatically, parents in rural Huining faced serious problems in financing their children's educational endeavors. Under these circumstances, siblings often turned into crucial supporters of their brothers' or sisters' higher education. While most university students perceived it as being just "natural" that their siblings supported them, they at the same time were very aware of the reciprocal obligation such support entailed.

Such was explained to me by Yu Lan, a university student who had lost her father in the aftermath of a serious traffic accident that had also left her older brother handicapped. Yu Lan seemed to worry little about how to repay her student loan after graduation. She expected her brother, who ran a comparatively successful local bus company, to support her in that respect:

Yu Lan: My debts do not pose a big problem. My brother earns cash. He will help me to repay my debts of about 20,000 yuan.

HO: Will he lend the money to you?

Yu Lan: No, he will not lend the money to me; he will give it to me. Relations in our family are very close. He will help me to repay the debt, but that does not mean that I will borrow the money from him. His help will be based on "feeling" (感情; *ganqing*), the "feeling of closeness" (亲感; *qingan*). Such feeling implies the principle of "if you help me now, I will help you at a later occasion." It means that one does not count the exact amount of money transferred. In other words, it implies that since you need my help and it is within the reach of my possibilities to help you, I will do so. Sometime in the future there will surely be an occasion when I will be in need of help and then I can expect you to help me within the reach of your possibilities. My brother has an income now, but compared to me he is clearly disadvantaged in terms of his lower educational level and his being physically handicapped. It is therefore very likely that in a few years I will be better off than him and that I will then have to help him.

Like in the other cases of rural Huining students who were financially supported by their siblings, a record of the exact amount of financial support received was said to be unnecessary, since between siblings debts would not be repaid in a direct and equivalent fashion anyway. Instead, the students claimed, receiving siblings' financial support evoked a deep gratitude, a "natural" feeling of obligation to help the supporter in return in the future. Since the future "return gift" was to be of higher value, it was needless to keep a nitpicking record of the initial financial transfers in the first place. A frequently quoted saying in this context employed the locally pertinent metaphor of water as a scarce resource: "The benevolence of being provided with a drop of water should be reciprocated with a bubbling fountain" (滴水之恩当以涌泉相报; *di shui zhi en dang yi tong quan xiang bao*). With respect to educational support, Tong Weibin, a recent graduate, summarized, "As a graduate you are very much aware that you owe your social position to other people's support. As long as you have a conscience (良心; *liangxin*, literally 'good heart'), you surely wish to reciprocate."

The Chinese language has a special term denominating the act of providing someone with the opportunity to study (供 . . . 上学; *gong . . . shangxue*). The use of the verb 供 *gong*—literally "to provide for" or "to offer sacrifice"—not only indicates the perception that education necessitates support but, moreover, denotes an act of giving that should be reciprocated. Distinct from the graduates of the early reform period, who had achieved socioeconomic mobility on the basis of a fully state-financed educational system (even though a supportive attitude of at least one family member surely had been indispensable), current students' and recent graduates' educational attainment was based on substantive financial contributions by particular supporters. In the village, the issue of educational support was constantly brought up in everyday conversations. Reminding the students and recent graduates of their supporters' contribution certainly aimed at inculcating feelings of gratitude and obligation to reciprocate.

The Confucian classics codify an explicit notion of reciprocity (报; *bao*) as the core principle of ethical conduct and proper social relationships (Yang 1957). Among Chinese, it has thus long been taken for granted that a good person always interacts with others in a reciprocal way (Yan 1996: 122, Yang 1957, Yang 1994). Such an ethic of reciprocity assumes a congruence between material exchange and the feelings that bind people together (Kipnis 1996). Material exchanges, such as giving a gift and doing a favor, are thus regarded not only as expressive of the good feelings between people but at the same time also as a way to create, maintain, acknowledge, or intensify such good feelings, since gifts "embody the desired closeness of a relationship, which they help to construct" (Kipnis 1997: 67). In view of such unity of emotional attachment and instrumentality, it is no contradiction that educational support may be motivated by both feelings of closeness and calculation of a future return.

When twenty-year-old student Wang Yalong at Lanzhou University explained to me why his sisters supported his education, he explicitly referred to the double nature of sibling support:

Wang Yalong: I pay my tuition with a student loan. For my living expenses, I depend on money sent from home. Basically all that money is provided by my two elder sisters. The eldest is already married, the second sister is about to get married soon. Since I went to senior high school, all my clothes and the money I needed has been provided for by my sisters. If we leave aside the role the feeling of closeness (亲情; *qinqing*, literally "kin feeling") plays, then I think their motivation is not only an emotional investment (感情投资; *ganqing touzi*), but also a monetary investment (金钱投资; *jinqian touzi*). We have this tradition (习惯; *xiguan*), and I feel it is very natural. My sisters provide me with the opportunity to study (供我上学; *gong wo shangxue*) and when I shall have money, as soon as I earn a little bit of money myself, I will surely give it to my parents or to my older sisters. Unless I become a person of bad character (变质了; *bianzhi le*) in the future . . . but I think I will not. [. . .] I think it will be like that, because of this feeling between us. There is a famous saying in Chinese to describe deep-felt gratitude 'carved into the bones and inscribed into the heart' (刻骨铭心; *ke gu ming xin*). That means if an incident leaves a deep impression on you and arouses really deep feelings, you will never forget it in your whole life.

Wang Yulong then talks specifically about his eldest sister:

> *HO*: Why do you think your sister gives you all that money?
>
> *Wang Yalong*: Well, one reason is maybe the close feeling between siblings, but she probably also has a [second] thought (有想法; *you xiangfa*). It is surely only a minor aspect, [but she thinks] when she helps me now, then later, when I will have work and a social position, I can help her, or I can help her son, my nephew. She probably thinks that way. But it is not her main motivation, the most important is still the good feelings between siblings, this feeling that you cannot measure with money. Between siblings there does not exist any borrowing of money. Other relatives could lend money for education, but between siblings we do not lend and borrow money.

By facilitating Wang Yulong's future access to resources, while at the same time strengthening his feelings of sibling relatedness and obligation to reciprocate the help received, his sisters' support was (also) a crucial strategy for securing his contribution to their own secure future, possibly in the form of him supporting their children's education. The case demonstrates that, irrespective of the supporter's original motivation being emotional, instrumental, or a mixture of both, the "dividends" of support are never direct returns on the monetary value involved but the relatedness that the transaction creates (Brandtstädter 2003). It is the relatedness that might pay off in the future.

Labor migrants could assume that their student siblings would feel a strong moral obligation to reciprocate the support they had received, since such support had been indispensable in facilitating their education. Moreover, even though the difficulties contemporary graduates face in the labor market does not guarantee that all of them will end up in high-level employment, graduates still can be expected to have access to an enhanced safety net they can access in times of emergency—for example, via former classmates. Helping to finance a sibling's education thus (also) served as an "investment" against future risks.

CONCLUSION

The diachronic view on sibling relatedness in rural Huining County during three decades of reform-socialist China demonstrated how government policies mediated sibling relatedness not only by impacting the size of sibling sets but also by shaping the conditions of socioeconomic mobility based on educational credentials. A closer look at education-related transactions between graduates and their siblings in the two historical periods, comprising three decades of post-Maoist reform, showed that far from solely diluting family resources, siblings played an important role in the provision of family support.

During the first two decades of reform socialism, when graduate employment still remained centrally planned, the education of a small minority of rural youth caused divergent life trajectories and decisive socioeconomic differences within the predominantly large sibling sets concerned. Graduates of this period, usually the only socially mobile actors in their sibling sets, often turned into important supporters for their siblings. Although not everybody followed the norm, many remained entangled in mutual dependencies with their rural siblings, almost like patrons with their clients. All graduates shared a general feeling of obligation to help their siblings in times of emergency. Moreover, they all faced a distinct moral obligation to contribute to the costs of their nieces' and nephews' educations. Since it was assumed that these nieces and nephews later would take good care of their elderly parents, graduates' "diagonal" intergenerational educational support was locally (also) interpreted as being ultimately targeted horizontally toward their siblings, while being accomplished indirectly via the next generation.

During the recent decade of reform policies, the impact of the family planning policy as well as the dramatic shifts in educational and labor policies toward increased marketization decisively changed local conditions of siblingship. Smaller sibling sets faced higher educational costs and insecure graduate labor markets, while siblings' (gendered) obligations of providing elderly care for the parents persisted. Sisters' financial contributions to their brothers' education were interpreted as reciprocation toward their parents for their upbringing. Between brothers, responsibilities of elderly care for the parents were assigned in accordance with each brother's actual living conditions. Young men's support for their brothers' education might thus (also) be motivated by the aim of alleviating their own future responsibility for providing care for their common parents.

In the poor rural region of Huining County, rising educational costs as well as high aspirations of participation in the national rush for economic development caused siblings' "fates" to become increasingly interdependent. Students and their migrant siblings both faced the pressure to organize their individual lives, which in the economically deprived region of rural Gansu province meant, above all, finding a pathway out of the locality. Increasing dependence on sibling support for realizing this goal seemed to strengthen rather than weaken sibling relatedness. Students were in great need of support from their siblings for realizing their educational aspirations and thus accumulated heavy reciprocal duties, while they at the same time faced the insecurities of the graduate labor market. Their migrant siblings often remitted some of their income to support their siblings' education, even though they themselves could expect to be in pressing need of financial means in the future, given the low level of income and short time spans of migrant labor employment. Their contribution to the financing of their siblings' education thus often went along with the hope of securing access to urban resources for themselves via the—hopefully—successful graduate siblings, who would feel obliged to reciprocate the help they had received.

In distinction to what some authors have argued about the disruptive impact of recent policies on kinship support in China, in the region where the fieldwork for this study was conducted, siblings were instead valued as reserves of support. Living on the bottom end of China's vast spectrum of socioeconomic disparities, the increasingly competitive environment did not turn siblings into competitors only. On the contrary, the interdependence of siblings' life trajectories made mutual sibling support decisive for individual and familial advancement. Certainly, increasing mutual dependency did not inhibit conflict between siblings, and it amplified the multiple pressures rural youth faced. Education-related sibling support also did not preclude utilitarian motivations on the part of the givers. Quite the contrary, in the insecure environment of contemporary China, investments in sibling relatedness through the "gift" of educational support just seemed to offer more in emotional and material terms than pure egotism. In their struggle for a decent and secure life, and for full participation in the country's rapid economic development, people in rural Huining County thus turned to their siblings as reserves of support—not least since they hardly had anybody else to turn to.

Presently, graduate unemployment has only become a pressing social problem in China the last decade. People in rural Huining thus still sustain hopes that higher education will eventually enable graduates to "change their fate," for themselves and for their siblings. However, if in the future expectations of education-based socioeconomic mobility decline, local experiences of sibling relatedness are likely to change as well.

ACKNOWLEDGMENTS

Data for this chapter was collected during one year of field research in Huining County in 2006–7. The project was conducted within the framework of the research group "Kinship and Social Support in China and Vietnam" at the Max Planck Institute for Social Anthropology (MPISA) in Halle, Germany. Field research was generously funded by MPISA. I thank all my informants in rural Huining for supporting my research. I have changed all personal names in the text to protect their privacy.

CHAPTER 6

TRANSNATIONAL MIGRATION AND CHANGES IN SIBLING SUPPORT IN GHANA

Cati Coe

International migration tends to result in translocal households located in two or more places, entailing the separation of kin from one another, whether husbands from wives, parents from children, or siblings from siblings. Despite the distance, kin remain connected through remittances, phone conversations, shipments of packages, and occasional visits. A growing literature is concerned with how this separation is affecting kinship ideologies and practice as a way of understanding what is new and different about contemporary global flows of people, goods, and wealth. The focus in this research literature, so far, has been on dyadic bonds between parent and child and between spouses (for example, Gamburd 2000; Hondagneu-Sotelo 1994; Levitt 2001; Olwig 1999; Parreñas 2004; Pribilsky 2007; Súarez-Orozco, Todorova, and Louie 2002). Siblings have been largely neglected in this literature, perhaps because scholars have operated from a Western model of the nuclear family, in which marital and parent-child relations are considered more intense than those involving siblings. However, communicating with, financially supporting, and receiving help from distant siblings are a significant part of migrants' transnational strategies, particularly in communities where siblings have historically had conceptual and practical importance (Drotbohm 2009, Olwig 2007). Even in communities where sibling relationships are not as profound, siblings can be a significant source of financial and emotional support for three reasons. For one, sibling relationships are potentially more long lasting than other familial relationships.[1] Second, they generate connection across personal differences, and finally, they are intertwined with significant relationships to parents, children, and spouses.

In some contexts, siblings are a more important relation than others, as Francis L. K. Hsu (1971) noted, although I do not consider any single dyadic relationship dominant in a society, nor should we lose sight of how dyadic relationships are embedded in wider social relations. Kin in Ghana are organized as lineages, divided into smaller "houses"—corporate units that comprise all the descendants of a common ancestor, including the living, the dead, and the unborn. Siblings—as the children of the same mother or father—are the primary building blocks of these larger patrilineal or matrilineal houses (Fortes 1969, Roth forthcoming). Through siblings—defined both more narrowly as the children of a birth parent and more widely as house members—children and adults experience a potentially broad social network of mutual support. Such mutual support systems are nurtured and modeled by sibling caretaking arrangements—in which an older child cares for a younger one—in childhood (Weisner 1982, Weisner and Gallimore 1977). In southern Ghana, lineage bonds—and siblings—have traditionally been more important than conjugal bonds, and women are more likely to turn to their brothers, and men to their sisters, than to their spouses for support and assistance (Bleek 1977, Fortes 1969). For example, when I interviewed a forty-eight-year-old woman in Akropong, a town in southern Ghana, about her life, she noted the normative obligation on siblings to provide assistance to one another: "*Sɛ wo nua wɔ hɔ na ne ho kyere no a, na wobetumi aboa no a, ɛsɛ sɛ woboa no.*" [If your sibling is in trouble and you can help, you have to help.] The number of birth and house siblings helps distribute economic gains and losses across a large group of people, evening out inequality between house members and reducing individual risk to job loss, starvation, or environmental change (Douglas 1971).

Other features of sibling relationships make them particularly valuable for mutual support. Siblings are in the same generation genealogically (Whyte et al. 2008), and compared to other family relations, siblings may be one of the more long-lasting relationships for an individual across his or her life span. Even though siblingship is a horizontal relationship genealogically (Kopytoff 1971), siblings can be differentiated from one another in other significant ways: by gender, age, and birth order. These differences between siblings mean that they encounter different opportunity structures or are at slightly different stages in their life courses, a situation that diversifies assets and minimizes risk across a set of siblings. Not only may parents be in different financial or social situations when their various children are born (Goody 1969), but siblings may have very different trajectories than one another as they age, ending up with differing amounts of social prestige, political power, and wealth, as the chapters by Helena Obendiek, Julia Pauli, and Erdmute Alber in this volume show. If siblings are far apart in age, as is usual in communities with high birth rates, siblings are not necessarily part of the same cohort or generation. A cohort, as a sociological concept, refers to a group of people sharing the same historical experience (such as structural adjustment reforms, free education, or war) at a similar stage of their life course—an event that affects their experiences and sense of self, and the opportunities available to them (Becker 1992, Elder and Caspi 1990; see also Olwig 2007). Karl Mannheim's definition of a generation is even stronger in that he emphasizes that such a group has a self-consciousness of itself as a distinct generation, such as baby boomers or depression-era children (1952 [1927]). Thus, although siblings are by definition members of the same generation in the genealogical sense, they might belong to different historical cohorts or generations in the Mannheimian sense (Whyte et al. 2008), because they do not always share the same historical experience, such that one brother may enlist and another may be too old or young to do so, or one may benefit from the expansion of secondary schools and another not, as in the case described by Obendiek in this volume. Nor do they have the self-consciousness of being in the same historical generation. In Ghana, the tension between the genealogical and historical senses of generation is what makes siblings so important to one another in mitigating the risks that life offers. Siblings are different—in terms of their stage in the life course as well as the variation in their life course trajectories—but obligated to one another as members of the same genealogical generation.

Although siblings are a significant relation in Ghana, to isolate them conceptually as a dyad is a mistake. A sibling is one of a host of ties in a person's life, and sibling relations are tied conceptually and practically to other kin relations, as well as nonkin relations like friends, as Sjaak van der Geest in this volume points out (see also Barth 1971, Kopytoff 1971, Minuchin 1985). As has been noted about family dynamics, "interactions between two people influence and are influenced by a third person. The response of each person to the other is conditioned by his or her joint relationship to a third person" (Elder and Caspi 1990: 221). Sibling relations operate similarly within a wider context of kinship, in which a sibling's support of another has repercussions for other generations. For instance, an older sibling may serve as a child nurse of a younger sibling, thus freeing up their mother to farm (Gottlieb 2004). Or, for an example of siblings affecting the generation after them, one form of mutual support between adult siblings in Ghana entails taking care of one or more of one another's children, termed *fostering* or *child circulation* in the anthropological literature of West Africa (Goody 1982, Isiugo-Abanihe 1985). Such fostering splits up siblings of the same mother or father, as one child goes to live with a sibling of a parent and the rest remain behind or go to other siblings of parents, but also creates new groups of siblings in the foster households. Furthermore, fostering can create a strong relationship between the child and his or her foster parent—the sibling of the child's parent—as well as strengthen the bond between siblings. For instance, adults have reported to me that as a result of a fostering relationship in their childhood, they ended up feeling closer to a sibling of a parent (their foster parent) than to their own biological mother or father. Another way that siblings can affect the next generation is the common scenario in Ghana in which an older sibling brings a younger sibling into his or her household, creating a strong bond between the older sibling's children and the younger sibling, who can function like an older sibling to his or her nieces and nephews (the case of the Namibian siblings described by Pauli in this volume). In a sense, as members of the same genealogical generation but several years apart in age, siblings can link genealogical and cohort generations. Mutual care can thus be provided stepwise through the generations, through older siblings' support of younger siblings and younger siblings' support of older siblings' children.

Furthermore, other relations affect sibling relations, such that we should not separate sibling relations from the larger universe of other relationships. As Sjaak van der Geest in this volume describes, a woman's close relationship with her husband can damage her relationship with her brother. Or, as had occurred with several grandmothers I met in southern Ghana, a grandmother can be overwhelmed by the care of grandchildren who are living with her, prompting one of her daughters to move her mother's foster children, most of whom are the children of the daughter's siblings, to her own household, raising them with her own children. A daughter's relationship with her mother thus results in her fostering her siblings' children. Claudia Roth (forthcoming) suggests from her work in urban Burkina Faso that the sibling set (of one mother) can step in to provide eldercare when the eldest son, who would be normatively responsible, cannot because of poverty. People's lives are interlinked across the generations and across their lifetimes, such that the making—or breaking—of a relationship in everyday life affects other relationships. Although the interdependence of relationships is often part of people's formalized and idealized conceptualization of kinship, these relationships' contingency on one another is also made manifest through the practice of everyday life (Carsten 2000). Individuals act in relation to one another in specific contexts, drawing on their understandings of the situation, internalized values, psychological responses, and the limitations and possibilities of their life circumstances.

Siblings' significance for individuals as a social safety net, their obligations to one another, and their influence on other generations are all factors that cause transnational migrants to rely on sibling relationships when they face difficulties abroad. Drawing on the different resources available in different national locations and relying on a broad network of support are ways of coping with the economic, legal, and social difficulties entailed in living and working abroad (Schmalzbauer 2008). The anthropological and sociological literatures on families and transnational migration have documented that many migrant parents rely on child fosterage arrangements to facilitate their migration, leaving behind or sending back their children to be cared for by extended family members (Gamburd 2000, Hondagneu-Sotelo and Avila 1997, Olwig 1999, Parreñas 2004, Yoshikawa 2011). While not focused on sibling relationships *per se*, this pattern challenges the

conventional narrative of modernity that extended family arrangements will disappear with capitalism and wage labor. Instead, evidence
seems to be building that extended family structures are well suited to
the increased mobility of labor in a global economy, helping sustain
the low wages paid to immigrant workers by lowering the costs of
maintaining nonworking family members (Jones 1992, Ong 1999).
Will sibling relationships become more important with globalization
and increasing international migration?

Although migration has long characterized West African social life,
international migration has significantly increased since the 1980s as a
result of structural adjustment programs and a decline in living stan-
dards for middle-class professionals and civil servants in the 1970s
and 1980s, generating a "new" and less elite culture of migration in
southern Ghana. Using available data, Ghanaian government statisti-
cian K. A. Twum-Baah (2005) estimates that with a population of 21
million Ghanaians resident in Ghana, another 1.5 million live outside the country, mostly in other parts of Africa rather than the most
prestigious destinations in Europe and North America. International
migration was once a sign of elite status, but it has become increasingly democratized, involving a broader swathe of the population,
including students, teachers, lower-level civil servants, and skilled
blue-collar workers like mechanics and electricians (Manuh 2006).
Still, international migrants from Ghana tend to be from the richer
southern part of the country and living in urban areas prior to their
migration (Adeku 1995).

This chapter will specifically focus on how international migrants
use their sibling relationships for help in caring for their children back
home. I will make two arguments in this regard. As alluded to before,
one is that international migrants are relying on their siblings in familiar ways as a transnational strategy because of constraints specific to
international migration: poor pay and housing conditions abroad;
limited childcare support abroad; or lack of authorization to bring
over their children. At the same time, because reliance on sibling
assistance is increasingly criticized discursively in Ghana, particularly
within the social milieu from which international migrants tend to
come, international migrants are reviving or extending a practice that
their compatriots at home are increasingly regarding less favorably as
an option of last resort. This ongoing social change at home means

that some international migrants depend on their siblings with ambivalence, resulting in the replacement of siblings with hired help. Focusing on sibling relationships in the context of transnational migration, then, highlights the process by which human agency creates and responds to social change, as people adapt kin relationships to new contexts and create new contexts out of existing expectations of kin.

EXPECTATIONS OF KINSHIP

To establish a baseline in regards to change over time, I will begin by discussing the childhood reminiscences of adults in their fifties and sixties in Akropong, a district capital of about 9,000 people, located in the Akuapem area of the Eastern Region of Ghana (Ghana Statistical Service 2002). These retrospective accounts come from a household survey I conducted in Akropong in 2008 to compare fostering among internal migrants to that among international migrants—that is, the fostering of children who had a parent elsewhere in Ghana with those who had a parent outside the country. Aiming for 90 interviews with the foster parents of children who had a parent abroad or a parent elsewhere in Ghana, based on a randomly generated list of numbers, I visited 220 houses across five different neighborhoods in the town of approximately 1,712 houses (not necessarily households), based on a satellite map available from the District Assembly. Ultimately, this effort resulted in interviews with 93 caregivers and with 80 of the children (ages eight to twenty-two) they were looking after, the overwhelming majority of these interviews conducted in Twi. Interviews with foster parents focused on their experience of raising the child as well as their own childhood experiences, to gain a sense of historical changes in family life.

Against this historical backdrop provided by foster parents' reminiscences, drawing on this same set of data, I will discuss how some parents and caregivers in Akropong criticize child fostering and advocate that parents raise their own children. I will then turn to the experience of international migrants and their children, drawing on several sources of data. One set of interviews came through a visit to Ghana in the summer of 2005, when I conducted focus group discussions with a total of forty-two students who had a parent or both parents abroad, in three secondary schools and one private school in southern Ghana. Two of the secondary schools and the private school were located in a metropolis of just over a million people (Kumasi); the third secondary school was located in Akropong, although most students came from large urban areas located about an hour away: the national capital Accra or the regional capital Koforidua. The focus group discussions occurred in school classrooms or meeting rooms without the presence of a teacher or another adult, and they were usually in English, at the students' request. Students were overly respectful in these settings but also responded to one another's complaints with their own, suggesting that these were common topics of discussion among themselves.

These discussions were followed up, where possible, with private interviews with children who had a migrant parent specifically in the United States. I visited twenty-nine of those students' guardians, with whom I had relatively short (half-hour) informal conversations, and I interviewed ten of those children's parents who were living in North America (one was in Canada; the rest were in the United States) in fall 2005. I have information about six additional families in Accra, Koforidua, and Kumasi through interviews with foster parents, birth parents, and the children themselves—contacts made through people I knew or through a Ghanaian church in the United States.

All the interviews and focus group discussions elicited adult and child discourses about family life and migration. The nature of the survey in Akropong ensured that these discourses came from a range of people reflecting the social composition of the town, particularly in terms of social class, ethnicity, and hometown origin. Although all the children were living in Akropong at the time, not all considered Akropong their hometown. Most of the children were Akan (from matrilineal families) and from somewhere in the Eastern Region, except for three children: one was Ga, one was Ewe, and one was Frafra (from the north)—the latter two patrilineal. In Kumasi, Koforidua, and Accra, similarly, most of the interviews were with people of Akan origin (Asante, Akyem, and Kwahu in particular), with a few Ewe and one Krobo, reflecting some of the ethnic diversity of southern Ghana. Quotations from interviews and focus groups are given in the language spoken (whether English or Twi), followed by a translation into English where necessary.

Through the perspectives of different people in the same families, I will give a sense of how sibling relationships are changing over time, particularly in response to transnational migration, in southern Ghana.

Siblings in the Childhoods of Akropong Residents

Siblings have historically been very important as potential caregivers for children and sources of help in Akropong, particularly in giving financial support for daily needs and in times of crisis. Mutual support both generates and indexes emotional bonds and trust between siblings. In Akropong, in previous generations, when people tended to have more children (six to ten children as opposed to the more common three to five children nowadays),[2] siblings varied widely in their ages. In some families, the eldest sibling was a young adult by the time the last one was born. Because of such differences, siblings could have very different childhood experiences; their connection was not based on shared experience but rather on "mutual affection and identification" and, particularly, "a bond of inescapable moral obligation to support one another against outsiders regardless of idiosyncrasies of personality and character" (Fortes 1969: 172). Erdmute Alber's chapter in this volume illustrates how this sense of moral obligation can be mobilized even when siblings do not know one another well. Furthermore, because of their differences in ages, siblings more widely spaced could be of more assistance to younger siblings, providing more direct assistance than is likely today, where siblings are fewer and more closely spaced.

Education has historically been important in Akropong, and even in the 1950s, in the childhoods of the people I interviewed, families tried to send their children to school, although girls were sent less often than boys. In large families, parents took care of the education of their older children, but by the time their younger children went to school, the parents were aging and unable to support the younger ones. As a result, while some children remained with their parents and were supported financially by older siblings, others went to live with their older siblings. In the latter situation, older siblings welcomed younger siblings' contribution to household labor, because the older siblings might be at a period in their lives where they were in the early stages of marriage and bearing young children, or just starting out in a career. The younger siblings helped their older siblings (or their siblings' spouses) combine family reproduction and economic activity by contributing to household work, their commercial work, and/or child care.

Rosina,[3] a sixty-year-old woman from Akropong, described this common experience in explaining to me why she was not educated beyond primary school. Her older siblings were educated, Rosina said, but by the time she and her younger siblings were ready for school, her father was an old man and could no longer farm as he used to, so there was no money to send her to school.

> *Na mεyε abɔfra kakra na me nua panyin no kɔ ware, na wɔn nso wɔkɔ akyin, ɔtontɔn ade nti na ɔwo a, na metu—na mete ne nykyεn na meturuw ne ba no ma no na watumi akɔ guaso. Na mεyε aduan ma mmɔfra no.*

When I was a little girl [about ten years old], my elder sister got married. She was a trader and she took things around to sell, so when she gave birth, I carried—I lived with her and carried her child on my back so she was able to go to the market. I made food for the children at home.

This scenario was relatively common, although, to her disappointment, Rosina was not sent to school through this fostering situation as many were, perhaps because school was less common for girls when she was a child and her elder sister as a trader needed her help during school hours.[4]

Older siblings may take in a favorite younger sibling, one who is old enough to be helpful, or one who needs help in some way. Although many adults and children said they loved all their siblings equally, Adelaide, a fifty-seven-year-old woman from Akropong, said that she loved her younger sister most of all: this is why her younger sister came to live with her when Adelaide was a young adult.

> *Na emu enuanom de, na me maame* last born *no εna na ɔno ne onipa a mepε n'asεm paa. Efi sε mekɔɔ Nkran no koraa no mebεfaa no kɔtenaa me nkyεn kɔpem sε ɔno nso kɔwie* form four *εwɔ me nkyεn ansa na ɔrefi me nkyεn. Enti* still *a mewɔ ɔdɔ wɔ ne mu.*

Among my siblings, the one whom I love is my mother's last born child. Even when I went to Accra [after finishing her apprenticeship as a seamstress], she came to live with me until she finished form four [the end of middle school], when she left me. I still have lots of love for her.

During the time that she lived with her, the younger sister helped Adelaide with her work as a seamstress, which she combined with baking on the side.

This mutual support between siblings can then be extended into the next generation, such that a fostered younger sibling like Rosina might then take in her elder sibling's children as she herself becomes an adult, out of gratitude for the support given. For instance, I met Prosper, an Ewe man in his seventies working in Akropong, who, as a child, had lived with his eldest brother. Four others among his older, educated siblings—three brothers and a sister—contributed to his school fees. Before the beginning of each school term, he described how he went from one sibling's home to another, spending a few days here, a week there, to collect the money he needed for the new term. "My sisters and brothers were caring for me," he said. "I was excited and I thought I had to learn hard, and repay them later in life." Because of his siblings' support for his education, Prosper was able to become a teacher. When he obtained his first posting as a newly minted teacher, he brought one of the sons of his eldest brother to live with him because he saw the boy was struggling with his education. The nephew was about twelve or thirteen years old and able to help Prosper, as a bachelor living alone, with the household chores. Prosper described his rationale for taking his nephew to live with him: "It strengthened my relationship with my eldest brother and the wife. Because I stayed with my eldest brother and wife throughout [my childhood], so I thought it was an opportunity to appreciate what they have done, and then try to bring up one of his children. Apart from trying to help him [the nephew] educationally, academically." Intergenerational support and mutual obligation therefore proceeded stepwise through siblings, with those in the prime of their adult working lives helping those ten or so years younger (whether in the next generation or a younger sibling) with material support in exchange for help with daily household labor. When the younger ones grow up and are employed, like Prosper, they may support the siblings who helped raise them, whether directly or in a more diagonal way, by giving them money in their old age or by taking care of their children, thus easing some of their cares.

When siblings in the first generation support one another by raising one another's children, siblings of the same mother or father in the second generation do not live together as children but rather have distinct experiences and affections as a result of their different caregivers and residences, schooling, and ages. Living with a parent's sibling may entail living with the children of that sibling, who would also be considered siblings.

At the same time, it is important to note that siblings who lived apart were not complete strangers to one another. No matter where a child resided, children, like adults, were very often in motion and traveling. Children were welcome in a number of households, and residential patterns were fluid. Children went to their hometowns for family celebrations, funerals, and festivals, sometimes meeting their mother, father, or siblings for the first time there, if they had been fostered since they were babies or toddlers. Others remained in more regular contact, visiting their parents, siblings, or other relatives on the weekends or during school holidays. A few adolescents went to boarding secondary school, prompting them to connect with their parents' siblings or other relatives who lived close to their school, whom they could visit on weekends or for a few days on vacation, before traveling the longer distance home. Such an environment creates, for a child, a wide network of potential support that can be activated in time of need, among the siblings of his or her parents, as well as among their children and his or her own siblings. Despite being fostered by her father's sister as a child and growing up with her children rather than her own siblings, Adelaide assured me, "*Seesei de yɛayɛ mpanyinfo a yehyia yɛn nyinaa yɛn ayɛ baako.*" [Now that we (my siblings and I) are grown up, when we meet, we are united.] Although separation of birth siblings is relatively common due to fostering, sibling unity and cooperation is highly valued, particularly as children mature and begin to exchange mutual support. Adelaide, you recall, had fostered her younger sister. However, the meaning of fostering and the accompanying division of child siblings among adult siblings of the parent is becoming increasingly critiqued and viewed as a sign of poverty or hardship.

Sibling Support as a Class Symbol

Given their potential for mutual support, across life stages and socioeconomic differences, we might think that siblings were particularly important today in evening out some of the social and economic inequality in contemporary Ghanaian life—inequalities heightened by urbanization, uneven opportunities for education, and global flows of goods, money, and people, as Obendiek describes in China (Goody 1982). Instead, among growing numbers of Ghanaians, in urban and periurban areas in southern Ghana, of different economic and educational levels, adult siblings are seen as an increasingly less significant source of support. Due to a Western model of parenthood that has been imported (Haukanes and Thelen 2010), some Ghanaians increasingly operate from a vision of a nuclear family living in a separate residence. Under this model of parenthood, they consider it important for siblings to live together in their childhoods, under the care of their parents, generating intimate bonds with one another and their parents within an enclosed space. Parent-child relations are gaining priority in childhood, over and above a broad network of support that could include the parents' siblings and their children. In adulthood, siblings are expected to operate independently from one another, establishing their own separate households and asking for support from one another only when in crisis.

A woman in her forties from Akyem who had married an Akropong man told me that when she married, her relatively wealthy family felt that her husband should support her, such that she did not feel that she could turn to her parents or siblings for help. Another woman, Shirley, in her thirties, raised in Koforidua and the wife of a secondary school teacher, emphasized that in her family there was an expectation that every sibling raise his or her own children, such that she would be reluctant to let a sister raise her own children. "*Enti obiara pɛ sɛ ɔbɛhwɛ n'adeɛ, mhmm, ɛna wobetumi ahwɛ w'adeɛ yiye ama wadu n'anim, saa!*" [Everyone wants to look after their own, to look after your own well so they attain higher heights—that is it!] Even so, her sister's adolescent daughter had come to stay with her. This was mutually beneficial in Shirley's eyes: the niece could attend her husband's secondary school as a day student, and her niece could help Shirley take care of recently born twins. But Shirley felt reluctant to let her own children go to live with her siblings, although she said that she might one day be in a situation where that would be the only option.

As Shirley's account suggests, while such a model of family life might seem familiar to Westerners, the nuclear family in Ghanaian ideology has far more permeable boundaries than it does in the West, with siblings and their children continuing to have rights and obligations—although far less than those due to one's children and parents. Urban elite and middle-class families will accept poorer and younger relatives in their households as house servants or as dependent relatives, pay for younger relatives' schooling, and send remittances back to their hometowns to help with relatives' funerals, support the siblings of parents, and contribute to family housing (Ardayfio-Schandorf and Amissah 1996, Oppong 1974). They are willing to foster-in the children of relatives, but they are reluctant to have their own children raised by others (see Alber 2004b for a similar situation in Benin). Fostering one's own child out to a sibling is increasingly critiqued and taken to be sign of desperation, poverty, or crisis. The positive reasons for fostering in the past included an ideology in which children would be better trained by a foster parent than a biological parent, or because the foster parent needed the help of someone, or because of the level of affection between the foster parent and the child.

Instead, today, the distribution of child siblings to the siblings of a parent is increasingly viewed as a survival strategy for families in crisis—whether due to divorce, death, or poverty—to distribute the burden of childcare to people who are more financially able and in more stable situations. Children therefore move from poorer households to relatively wealthier ones. Giving out one's children to live with others—siblings or nonrelatives alike—is increasingly stigmatized in Akropong, because it is associated with servitude, poverty, and the possible mistreatment of children. Many parents, particularly younger and more educated people, aim to raise their children themselves, if they can, without asking for siblings' support. In discussing fostering with a friend of mine, a woman in her fifties who sold used clothes, she stated with great energy, "*Ɛfa kɛse no yɛ ahokyerɛ na ɛma obi de ne ba kɔma obi sɛ ɔne no tena. Sɛ anka ɛnyɛ ahokyerɛ de a, ɛyɛ me sɛ obiara nni hɔ a, ɔbɛwo ne ba sɛ womfa no nkɔ ntena.*" [A large cause that makes someone send his or her child to live with someone else is poverty. If there was no poverty, it seems to me that no one would send a child he or she has given birth to away to live [elsewhere].] This statement was particularly poignant because, barely making ends meet as a single mother, she worked hard to fund her daughters' education, suggesting that her passion about this matter came from her own closeness to the situation she described. She commented that many cases of fostering in the town occurred because the parents did not have work or because one parent had died, which supported what other people told me. Although fostering in the past was used for a wide variety of reasons, given the contemporary idealization of parents as the best caregivers, inabilities on the part of parents to take care of their children are now cited much more often as the reason.[5] As Jennifer Hirsch (2003) has demonstrated in her work on Mexicans' expectations of love and marriage, changes can be occurring in family life independently of transnational migration. Within this complicated, changing set of expectations and concerns concerning siblings, international migrants are asking for support from their siblings back home to raise their children, although some do so with great ambivalence.

Siblings in Transnational Families

Although international migrants are sometimes viewed as breaking away from "tradition" through their migration, the literature instead finds a mixed picture in which migrants also uphold more traditional gender roles (Gamburd 2000) or their remittances fuel local celebrations (Martinez 1993, Small 1997). Likewise, Ghanaian international migrants find themselves turning to "traditional" sibling support in raising their children. Their reasons have little to do with poverty, for most migrants are better off than their relatives in Ghana simply by virtue of the exchange rate between the US dollar, the euro, or the Nigerian naira and the Ghanaian cedi. According to the current logic, in which children go to live with more stable or wealthier adults, international migrants should be bringing their siblings' children to live with them abroad, giving them access to schools abroad, rather than leaving behind or sending back their own children in their siblings' care in Ghana. However, international migrants have trouble fostering their siblings' children for the same reasons that they have difficulty raising their own. They find that immigration regulations make it hard to bring over their children, requiring a delay of many years before applications are processed and approved. Others find it difficult to combine employment with childcare; for some, this is a concern with the quality of commercial daycare, and for others, a concern about the cost of such childcare (Coe 2012). Care for a migrant's children left behind is only one of several responsibilities given to siblings in Ghana, which can further include taking care of elderly parents or overseeing the building of a migrant's house and business investments (Mazzucato 2008). In return, migrants send remittances to their siblings and, if they have a house, provide housing for their siblings and their families. They may also help their siblings start a small business. As has been noted in Cape Verdean transnational families (Drotbohm 2009), fostering between siblings helps maintain the connection between them.

Siblings are particularly valued by international migrants, as by other Ghanaians, as foster parents. Although grandmothers are a common foster parent in Akropong, as is the case in other parts of West Africa (for example, Alber 2004b, Bledsoe and Isiugo-Abanihe 1989, Notermans 2004), they are considered poor disciplinarians. Perceived as physically weak and indulgent to their grandchildren, grandmothers are apt to raise spoiled and misbehaving children, according to many Ghanaians. Siblings, more likely to be in the prime of their lives, are considered physically strong and more likely to raise their siblings' children like their own children, with firm discipline and good training. I asked Joanna, a young woman who had recently joined her father in the United States, to consider whether she would send her future children to Ghana to be raised, in light of her own experiences as a "left-behind" child. She thought it would be a good idea, but it depended on her relatives back home.

> *Joanna:* You need good family. I can't just send my child to anyone. My mom will probably spoil him or her, but—*she laughs*—I hope my brothers or someone who is in a good position. Grandparents are good but they just spoil kids. *She laughs.*
> *Cati:* Whereas your brother would not?
> *Joanna:* I don't think so. If anything happens, he'll say—*switching to a deep, gruff voice*—"Hey no. Not here." Whereas the grandparent will say—*switching to a singsong voice*—"Oh, that's my grandbaby." *She laughs.*

International migrants are, then, reanimating dependence on siblings and other family members to care for their children, despite the growing critique of out-fostering in urban, middle-class circles from which many international migrants come.

However, migrants are creating several changes and pressures in fostering practices as a result, with an accompanying shift in sibling dynamics. Rather than children being scattered among various siblings of the parents, or one sibling taking care of another's child, some international migrants make a strong attempt to keep their children together in one household. Furthermore, unlike other fostering-out parents, who feel somewhat indebted and grateful to the foster parent, international migrants tend to be in a position of power and wealth over the foster parent, who may well be dependent on the migrant's remittances and seek to do the migrant's bidding. One sign of this is that while some children of international migrants move to the foster parent's household, as occurs traditionally, in other cases the foster parent moves to live with the children, sometimes in a new city, into the house that the international migrant has built or provides. Because of the differential power and wealth between siblings in the midst of mutual obligation, there can be considerable tension over remittances and child-raising strategies, although similar conflicts can also occur between siblings who remain in Ghana.

Because of concerns about conflicts over care, some migrants shy away from relying on their siblings in this way and instead employ nonrelatives as foster parents, or paid care givers. Anita, a longtime resident in New York, talked about her decision to raise her four children in the United States. Her mother had died, and her sister living in Ghana had her own children, so Anita felt that there was no one to send them to. She did not want to burden her sister: even if she sent money home, she felt it would still be a responsibility on someone else to look after her kids. Anita wanted to send the children to boarding school in Ghana, but she didn't want to place a burden on a teacher to look after them either. So she raised them in the United States, despite trepidations about its effects on their moral behavior. Some international migrants seek to resolve these tensions by turning to paid caregivers, including boarding schools, so that they have more control over the child-raising situation and can maintain harmonious relationships with their siblings.

For other international migrants, out-fostering by those abroad is a natural extension of existing practices of child fostering and mutual support between siblings in Ghana. To return to Prosper's situation, the support between brothers has even extended into the third generation: the grandson of Prosper's eldest brother is a teenage boy who attends boarding school near to where Prosper lives and who stays with Prosper on school holidays. The boy and his sister used to live with his mother, until she traveled with her new husband to the United Kingdom. The boy's sister now lives with her maternal grandmother in the regional capital of Koforidua. Prosper's nephew, the boy's father, visits Prosper regularly from Accra, bringing food and other items to help him out, and seeking advice and discussing his son's academic progress with Prosper. The chain of mutual support established in Prosper's childhood continues to add links as new generations are born and grow up, extending to the children of international migrants.

Similarly, Godfried, a civil servant in Kumasi from the town of Mampong in the Ashanti Region, raised his two youngest siblings, the ninth- and tenth-born, when they were in their teens after their mother in common died. As a responsible older brother, Godfried paid for their schooling through the end of secondary school. His own two children were then living in Mampong with their mother, from whom he had separated. A year after Godfried emigrated to the United States, he asked his younger sister (the ninth-born), then only twenty years old, to bring his oldest son, then age twelve, to live with her in the city of Kumasi, because he was worried about his son's education in the care of the boy's mother. After a divorce, some fathers take boys under their care as they grow older, and this seemed to be happening in Godfried's case. Godfried's sister explained to me that Godfried told her that he had chosen her to raise his son, despite her youth, because he knew what she was like, having raised her. He trusted her the most, she said, out of their siblings. Even though he struggles to work without authorization and has a new family in the United States, Godfried continued to support his sister with remittances, which allowed her to open a small kiosk selling provisions in a suburb of Kumasi. She chose a private school for his son in the neighborhood, after asking acquaintances about the local schools.

Likewise, Lydia had brought her younger sister to live with her when she was working as a trader in Kumasi. When she married in Kumasi, she and her younger sister "came as a package," joked Lydia's husband to me in their apartment in the Bronx, a neighborhood in New York City. After her marriage, Lydia gave birth to a daughter, her husband emigrated abroad (to various countries in succession, before ending up in the United States), and she continued to live with her younger sister in Kumasi. When Lydia joined her husband abroad in the United States, she left behind their thirteen-year-old daughter with her younger sister, now a seamstress in her twenties, whom I met in Kumasi. Lydia's husband noted that his daughter probably knew her mother's sister better than her mother, since she had lived with her all her life. Lydia and her husband also supported other younger siblings on both sides by letting them live in the house Lydia's husband had built in a suburb of Kumasi.

As a fourth example of the relatively smooth extension of fostering to support international migrants, in Akropong, Jane took in her sister's son, Kwabena, when he was sixteen months old, so that her sister could train and then work as a seamstress in Accra. When her sister later married a Ghanaian migrant to the United Kingdom and joined him there, the sister left Kwabena behind with Jane. Although Kwabena's mother plans to bring him to the United Kingdom eventually, in the meantime, her sister and her son (now fifteen years old) have grown quite attached to one another, such that Jane is wistful when she talks about his leaving. Although Kwabena is excited to go to Britain, as are many children in Akropong, he also does not miss his mother but is content with the situation, in which his mother calls him regularly and sends him clothes occasionally, and in which his mother's sister and her husband take good care of him.[6]

Other fostering situations do not work out as smoothly as these examples. One woman in her twenties, now living in the United States, described how she and her three brothers lived in their parents' house in Kumasi with their mother's younger sister after their mother, a civil servant in a regional education office, joined their father, a former contractor, in the United States:

Afua: We didn't go to live with our aunt; she actually moved.
Cati: To stay with you?
Afua: Yes. Because we had a big house and everything. My mom, my parents were actually paying for her rent and everything; she wasn't spending her money on anything.
Cati: And they were sending money back to pay for you and of course that was paying for her food and other things?

> *Afua*: She never had to use anything, her money, on us, anything. [My mother] asked the question, "Who do you want [to live with you when I emigrate]?" And looking at her family, this particular aunt was the youngest. And before, we used to be very close to her. She had actually stayed with us before. . . . And we were very connected to her in so many ways. She was a teacher; she would teach us stuff. We actually liked her. So that was the first name that came [up in our conversation about who to ask to stay with us].

Through her connections at the education office, Afua's mother was able to arrange her younger sister's transfer from a school in a remote village to one in Kumasi so that she could take care of Afua and her brothers in their own house. Because of the sister's youth and unmarried status, she could be flexible in changing her living situation, particularly in moving to an urban area where there were greater comforts and opportunities, and grateful for the remittances that her older sister would send. Her background as a teacher suggested that she could help with the children's studies. The children knew her from when she had lived with them prior to becoming a teacher. Despite these good omens, however, the care-giving relationship between the mother's sister and the children deteriorated rapidly once the mother's sister married and had children herself. They also lived together for a much longer period of time than initially anticipated, when the children's visa applications ran into difficulties. Afua described the effect of her parents' migration on her and her two younger brothers. Because her mother's sister did not take good care of them, "It was more like each one for himself. You do whatever you have to do to survive. And that was really hard." She described not sharing food with her siblings, symbolizing the lack of unity. Afua felt that she was emotionally distant from her brothers even though they lived together because of the tense atmosphere in the house.

Other migrants weigh such stories, shared through the diasporan grapevine, in their decisions about how to raise their children. Cecilia, a middle-aged woman from Kwahu who had been a trader in Accra and had lived in the United States for eight years, explained why she first turned to hired help, rather than her sisters in Ghana, to care for her three children there: "Sometimes you don't want to turn to family, because they might do something to hurt you. If a stranger treats you badly, it doesn't hurt so much, because you expect it. Plus, these family hurts could ruin the relationship between the cousins," by which she meant her sisters' children and her own. Cecilia's comment reveals her level of mistrust about kin relations and a concern about whether her siblings have her best interests at heart, at the same time as she wants to maintain sibling unity and connection through the generations.[7] A stepsister who was a teacher eventually persuaded Cecilia that the hired care giver was not doing a good job and moved herself into Cecilia's house in Accra, where Cecilia's children lived, with her own three adolescent children and her own foster child, who did much of the household work. Although she is an undocumented worker in the United States and has limited employment prospects, Cecilia tries to pay for the education of all her sisters' children, not just those of the sister fostering her children, so that they will not be jealous of the remittances she sends to the sister who fosters her children.

Mary went the opposite direction, beginning with a sister's care and then turning to hired help when she decided that her sister's care of her eight-year-old son was inadequate, after he repeated several grades at school. Mary felt that one of the reasons for his poor academic performance was that her sister did not have the time to supervise his homework after school. Mary's sister had seemed ideal as a care giver: she was a teacher and lived in Koforidua, a regional capital, where many private schools were available. However, Mary's sister was burdened by household chores and her own employment: she had three children, aged five to thirteen, and her husband was a teacher who worked in another town far away, so that he was only home on weekends. Because Mary felt that her sister could not adequately supervise her son's homework, Mary brought her son to live in her mostly completed house on the outskirts of Accra and asked an old friend, a kindergarten teacher, to live there; she paid her salary in lieu of her friend going to work.[8] Enrolling him in a nearby private school, she hoped that her son's academic performance would improve.

International migrants find themselves in a situation where the support of siblings would be beneficial, particularly in helping raise children whom it is impossible or difficult to bring abroad. Such support is both an extension of sibling mutual support known from migrants' child and adult experiences *and* new. It is an extension because it draws on experiences of siblings' fostering the next generation, with the expectations of generalized reciprocity that such fostering entails. It is new because the dynamics have changed, such that more power and wealth rests with the migrant parent than with the foster parent, making relations between siblings more fraught, shaped by jealousy and lack of trust. Furthermore, many migrants come from an urban context where it is expected—except in cases of crisis—that parents raise their own children, in order to ensure their academic preparation and good character, thus making migrants concerned about placing such a burden on their siblings.

CONCLUSION

Siblings are an important source of mutual support for people in Ghana because siblingship is a long-lasting relationship in which people are at slightly different stages of the life course and with access to different resources and opportunities. Of the same generation genealogically, siblingship is useful because it links across cohorts and generations in the sense presented by Karl Mannheim. Although the significance of siblings in southern Ghana might seem to support Hsu's notion of a dominant dyad that provides the model for other relationships, it is more the case that sibling relations operate within a larger social context, such that they affect and are affected by other relations. For example, one source of mutual support between siblings is fostering. Fostering one another or one another's children generates new intimacies through shared experiences between siblings and, in the next generation, between siblings' children. Siblings can also raise one another or one another's children to save their parents from the task. In the childhoods of previous generations, older siblings paid for the schooling of their younger siblings, who then, in turn, helped raise the older siblings' own children. Support thus flowed stepwise through the generations and cohorts, in which people supported those who were about ten or so years younger, whether such support came directly from siblings or was mediated through the sibling's children. For example, Godfried raised his younger sister, who is now, in her early twenties, raising his son because of his migration to the United States. It is the combination of connection across differences (in age and available resources) that leads siblings to be in a position of being helpful to one another, and through one another, to the previous or next generation.

Such mutual support between siblings, while still commonly practiced, is increasingly being critiqued, as drawing on a broad base of support from the extended family is associated with poverty, familial crisis, and death. New models of family life stress the significance of the nuclear family living together, supporting itself and possibly some poorer and more dependent members of the extended family. Middle-class and elite families are willing to foster-in the children of their siblings but are reluctant to foster their own children out. Fostering is increasingly associated with a child's potential mistreatment and exploitation. The critique of fostering among middle-class, urban Ghanaians complicates the strategies for migrants, who would like to maintain a middle-class identity for themselves and their children.

When Ghanaians go abroad, like other immigrants, they face situations that cause them to turn to their relatives and reestablish elements of their home communities abroad, through religious worship (D'Alisera 2004) or hometown associations (Attah-Poku 1996). With work—as taxi drivers, home health aides, and retail workers—consuming their time abroad and immigration laws making it difficult to bring over family members who might provide household support, transnational migrants desire the interdependence and mutual support of siblings. Given the nuclear family's association with modernity, we might expect siblings to become less significant. Instead, because of restrictive immigration regimes and lack of social support for children in the United States (Coe 2008), migrants are reviving practices of kinship that are familiar from their lived experience, but critiqued, by mobilizing transnational relationships with adult siblings. For some, reliance on siblings in Ghana is an extension of stepwise processes that have been ongoing in their families already. However, for those who have been living according to the newer model of a nuclear family, sibling dependence, prompted by a parent's migration, looks and feels more problematic. In both situations, fostering differs from traditional forms of fostering because of the status and wealth of the fostering-out (migrant) parent in comparison to his or her siblings.

Not all migrants are making the same decisions about raising their children; rather, their decisions are tempered by their siblings' situations, their own childhood experiences, and their legal status abroad, among other factors. However, despite these differences, they are engaging in an ongoing cultural conversation in Ghana and abroad about the significance of siblings for mutual support in their adult lives and for their children.

Acknowledgments

I am grateful to all those who were willing to be interviewed for this project as well as the rest of my research team: Kweku Aryeh, who assisted with the interviews; Joe Banson and Margaret Rose Tettey, who cofacilitated the children's focus group discussions; and Rogers Krobea Asante, Joe Banson, Bright Nkrumah, and Emmanuel Amo Ofori, who worked on the transcriptions. All provided advice at crucial points. The research was financially supported by the National Science Foundation, the Council on the Development of Social Research in Africa (CODESRIA), and the Wenner-Gren Foundation for Anthropological Research. My thanks to Erdmute Alber, Tatjana Thelen, Sjaak van der Geest, and an anonymous reviewer for excellent comments on an earlier draft of this paper.

Afterword

Janet Carsten

It is a pleasure to read this timely and ethnographically rich collection of essays, which amply documents the fruitfulness of viewing kinship through the lens of sibling relationships. Not only are sibling ties often the longest-lasting kinship connections of life but, as all the contributors emphasise, they necessarily take different forms in different phases of the life course and thus provide an opportunity to examine the processual nature of kinship connections (see also Davidoff 2012). As well as being emblematic of similarity, equality, and unity, siblingship encompasses principles of differentiation through age and gender distinctions, and this diverging set of possibilities is shown in all the essays. In fact, siblingship may simultaneously encapsulate the apparently contradictory principles of closeness and distance, similarity and distinction, equality and hierarchy. It is thus perhaps a uniquely flexible relation and one with myriad potential for symbolic as well as practical elaboration and extension. Idioms and practices of siblingship may apply to half- and step relations as well as to cousins and friends. Not surprisingly, therefore, this volume demonstrates how relations of siblingship are mobilised in a remarkable range of contexts and ways.

The longevity of sibling relations has important consequences. Long after parents have ceased to be able to provide for their children, adult siblings are often a source of material and moral support to one another. And significantly, the essays in this volume show how this flow of "goods" may continue down the generations with support to the children of siblings continuing, reciprocating, or standing in for what has been given to, or received from, brothers or sisters. As several authors point out, this implies that siblingship cannot simply be considered as a horizontal relationship within one generation. In some cases, this "multigenerational" effect of siblingship is expressed in relationship terminologies that are elaborations of sibling terms. Kinship terminologies may not only highlight the principle of siblingship but also imply that intergenerational relations are derived from ties between siblings (see, for example, Carsten 1997, McKinley 1981).

The intergenerational continuity of siblingship has implications for available avenues of support, but it also means that relationships between siblings are likely to be entangled with other kinds of ties in complex ways. Several of the essays here show how siblingship's capacity to be a resource for support may come into conflict with the expectations of spouses and affines. Once married, adult siblings may be considered to have obligations to their own spouses and children that override those to their brothers or sisters. This makes clear how the importance of siblingship emerges in the context of other kinship relations (rather than simply offering an alternative to the classic anthropological tropes of alliance and descent). It also demonstrates how relations between brothers and sisters also contain the seeds of tensions, conflict, rivalry, and competition—and this often becomes particularly evident during contested processes of succession and inheritance (see also Lambek 2011).

Several of the essays emphasize the experiential dimensions of siblingship—which, once again, may have a long afterlife. Shared memories of childhood are one aspect of a wider sharing between siblings that is discussed in the introduction to this volume and may constitute an emotional resource into adulthood. But conversely, siblings who have been treated differently in childhood and who have not grown up together (as is often the case) may not only be less close as adults; their differential treatment may also foster conflict or jealousy between them. When the different opportunities and pathways taken by different members of a sibling set serve to create economic or social distinctions between them, the potential for conflict—as well as the opportunities for aid—may be heightened. Interestingly, the theme of fosterage is highlighted in many of the essays here. As the siblings of parents are often particularly favored foster parents or may have explicit rights to the children of their siblings, the cooccurrence of the themes of siblingship and fostering is hardly coincidental.

And this once again illuminates the entanglements of hierarchical obligation, emotional closeness, and solidarity or unity that may be encompassed by siblingship.

The essays reveal another theme that might provide an inspiration for further scholarship. Apparently, the remarkable flexibility of siblingship lends itself particularly well to adaption to new forms of socioeconomic context. The scenarios of transnational migration and flexible labor or of changing state policies toward education or fertility considered here show how siblingship is amenable to being adapted to provide resources in new ways. But alongside the evidence of how siblingship is affected by state policies, we might also ask how siblingship impacts the state. With what practical or metaphorical resources does siblingship endow the state? What is the significance of symbolic idioms of siblingship in political life? In what practical ways do expectations about ties between siblings impact state policies? And what are the wider implications of decreasing fertility and increasing proportions of one-child families (which may themselves partly be the outcome of state interventions) for state policies and institutions?

Reversing, or complicating, the apparently obvious order of scale and priority between the family and state may remind us that the separation of a familial domain from the political is part of the ideology of modernity rather than its lived reality (see Cannell and McKinnon 2013). We should not assume that, in contexts of modernity, it is the state that acts on kinship rather than the other way round (Carsten 2007). But this might also provide the counterpoint to another potentially fruitful reversal. The authors in this volume remark on the apparent lack of attention paid to siblingship in anthropological studies of kinship. As they acknowledge, the record from Oceania and Southeast Asia is perhaps something of an exception here. While it might seem obvious from a European or North American vantage point—in which ties of filiation tend to be given priority over siblingship—that parents produce sibling sets, a Malay or Indonesian perspective suggests that this priority can be turned around. In the Malay world, one might just as well say that it is sibling sets that produce parents—and this is often elaborated in myth, in stories about past migration, in kinship terminology, and in the way young children are encouraged to behave toward their siblings (Carsten 1997, Errington 1989).

This insight from the ethnography has the potential to alter not just how we view siblingship but also our understanding of the nexus of relationships within which siblingship takes its place. In this way the generative possibilities of siblingship that are suggested by these essays have not yet been exhausted.

CONTRIBUTORS

Erdmute Alber is professor of social anthropology at the University of Bayreuth (Germany). Her research in Benin, conducted since 1992, includes the anthropology of power and the state as well as kinship, childhood, child fostering, and intergenerational relations. She is the author of *Im Gewand von Herrschaft: Modalitäten der Macht bei den Baatombu (1895–1995)* (2000) and a coeditor of *Generations in Africa: Connections and Conflicts* (2008). She is the editor of the journal *Sociologus* and vice-dean of the Bayreuth International Graduate School of African Studies. Currently, she is finishing a book manuscript on child fostering in northern Benin.

Janet Carsten is professor of social and cultural anthropology at the University of Edinburgh (United Kingdom). Her research, based in Malaysia and Britain, launched a more processual approach to kinship and relatedness. She is the author of *The Heat of the Hearth* (1997) and *After Kinship* (2004), and the editor of *Ghosts of Memory: Essays on Remembrance and Relatedness* (2007), *Cultures of Relatedness: New Approaches to the Study of Kinship* (2000), and (with Stephen Hugh-Jones) *About the House: Lévi-Strauss and Beyond* (1995). Currently, she is completing a book manuscript on articulations between popular and medical ideas about blood in Malaysia.

Cati Coe is an associate professor of anthropology at Rutgers University, Camden (United States). Her research in Ghana, conducted since 1997, has focused on cultural politics, youth, and transnational migration. She is the author of *The Dilemmas of Culture in African Schools: Youth, Nationalism, and the Transformation of Knowledge* (2005) and a coeditor of *Everyday Ruptures: Children, Youth, and Migration in Global Perspective* (2011). Her book *The Scattered Family: Parenting, African Migrants, and Global Capitalism* is forthcoming in late 2013, and she is beginning work on a new project on African immigrants working in the field of eldercare.

Helena Obendiek is a sinologist and anthropologist. She has worked on kinship, gender, education, ethnic relations, material culture, and rural development in China. She is the author of *The Tarim Basin Carpet: A Tradition in Transition* (China Heritage Arts Foundation, 1997). From 2006 to 2010 she was a member of the focus group on "Kinship and Social Support in China and Vietnam" at the Max-Planck Institute for Social Anthropology in Halle, Germany. Currently she is preparing to publish the results of her related field research in rural Gansu Province, China. She is employed as a student advisor and international coordinator at Konstanz University of Applied Sciences in Konstanz (Germany).

Julia Pauli is a professor of social and cultural anthropology at Hamburg University (Germany). Her main research interests are gender and kinship studies, anthropological demography, transnational migration, consumption and class formation processes. She has done extensive fieldwork in Mexico (since 1995) and Namibia (since 2003). She is the author of *The Planned Child: Demographic, Economic and Social Transformations in a Mexican Community* (in German, 2000) and is currently completing a book manuscript tentatively titled *Celebrating Distinctions: Marriage Transformations and Elite Formations in Rural Namibia.*

Sjaak van der Geest is emeritus professor of medical anthropology at the University of Amsterdam (Netherlands) and member of the Amsterdam Institute of Social Science Research (AISSR). He has done fieldwork in Ghana and Cameroon on a variety of subjects, including kinship and conflict; sexual relationships and birth control; the use and distribution of medicines; popular song texts; the meanings of growing old, death, and dying; concepts of dirt and hygiene; hospital life; and the anthropology of the night. He is founder and editor-in-chief of the journal *Medische Antropologie* and assistant editor of several other journals in the field of medical anthropology. His personal website is at http://www.sjaakvandergeest.nl.

Tatjana Thelen is professor for ethnographic methods and social network analysis at the University of Vienna (Austria). Her research interests include kinship, generational relations, social security, and care. Among other projects, she directed the anthropological research within the comparative project KASS (Kinship and Social Security, sponsored by the European Union). She coedited *Parenting after the Century of Child: Travelling Ideals, Institutional Negotiations and Individual Responses* (2010) and is currently working on a book manuscript on practices of care as ways of establishing and reproducing different kinds of meaningful relations.

NOTES

CHAPTER 1

1. Grandparenthood constitutes another missing theme in the kinship debates that has recently been discovered as a fruitful research theme (Bledsoe and Isiugo-Abanihe 1989; Geissler, Whyte, and Alber 2004; Thelen 2005; Attias-Donfut and Segalen 2007; Thelen and Leutloff-Grandits 2010).

2. The psychological and psychoanalytic literature has historically emphasized the parent-child bond. However, there is some attention paid to personality development in childhood, because birth order, family size, and sibling gender status seemed to generate different responses to sibling rivalry (for examples, see Adler 1924, Sutton-Smith and Rosenberg 1970). As G. N. Ramu (2006) notes, these studies of sibling rivalry had serious flaws, as they were drawn from retrospective accounts by adults. Research in the 1980s began to focus on actual interactions between siblings in early childhood and adolescence, showing that rivalry was only one aspect of siblinghood, which also included friendship and alliances against parents and others (Goetting 1986). Interactional studies also highlighted the role children played in one another's social, emotional, and cognitive development by helping children learn to deal with a full range of behavior, including aggression and threats (for example, Pepler, Abramovitch, and Corter 1981), and to develop the perspective of others (Dunn and Kendrick 1982). The psychological literature has tended to focus on siblings in childhood and the conflict between them as important elements in their socialization and personality development; in contrast, the anthropological literature has historically centered on siblingship in adulthood and on their similarity based on shared parentage and generation.

3. Anthropological studies of siblings in childhood showed that older siblings typically play an important role in socialization, in

complex ways, even when they are not accorded a formal child-minding role (Zukow 1989). Older siblings mediate between the generations by carrying out both peer-like and parent-like activities for younger siblings (Ervin Tripp 1989).

4. See also Marshall 1983: 3.

5. Shared parentage tends to be the dominant Western construction, and some authors go to great length to differentiate between different sorts of siblings (Sanders 2009: 2) On variability of the construction in European history, see Johnson and Sabean 2011.

6. Although Janet Carsten puts siblingship in relation to the house in Langkawi (and more widely in Southeast Asia) at the center of her analysis, her focus is on their interconnection and not as much on the sibling relation itself.

CHAPTER 2

1. All names are pseudonyms.

2. I thank Cati Coe and Tatjana Thelen for terminological and conceptual inspiration.

3. That I compare these two research settings is not only due to their similarities in terms of migration and household patterns. The comparison is also linked to my personal research history. Because of my long-term fieldwork in both areas, I am well acquainted with the ethnographic details and personal histories. To trace only two cases of sister relations over time allows me to embed and interpret the cases in detail within their wider cultural context (see Alber, this volume, for a similar argument). However, focusing on only two detailed case histories has the drawback of producing potential biases, especially regarding the selection of the analyzed cases. For example, the two sister pairs presented here are composed of older sisters who are close in age. Although it is impossible to eliminate these biases given my case-based approach, I will highlight when interpretations result from my specific approach and perspective. Overall, however, the life histories and life circumstances of the four women introduced here are exemplary of the lives of other women their age in the two communities.

4. For more information on my Mexican research, see Pauli 2000, 2008.

5. For more information on the Namibian research, see Pauli n.d., 2009, 2012.

6. In 2004, the community Fransfontein had 137 households. Another 161 households were located on the adjacent communal grazing area (Pauli n.d., 2009: Chapter 2).

7. Recombinant families in western Europe may also be an interesting site for further research on growing up together and sibling ties (see Pauli 2006).

8. Although ethnic identity and belonging are problematic issues in post-Apartheid Namibia, they remain central topics in everyday life. Most people speak Khoekhoegowab and according to an ethnographic census we took in July 2004 consider themselves as Damara (63 percent), followed by Herero (13 percent) and Nama (9 percent).

9. The same logic just described for siblings also applies to Ego's mother's and father's generation. The siblings of Ego's parents with the same gender as the parent (mother's sister and father's brother) are also termed *parents*. Consequently, for the mother's sister, the children of her sister are also classified as her children.

10. Here differences between our models of parenthood and childhood compared to those of our Fransfontein interlocutors become visible (see Thelen and Haukanes 2010).

11. A similar observation is mentioned by Cati Coe in her study of Ghanaian transnational families (Coe 2008: 245).

12. My use of the term *key experience* has been inspired by Sherry Ortner's reflections on *key symbols* (Ortner 1973).

13. The opposite applies as well. Petra, a Fransfontein woman in her late twenties, discussed with me her relation to Herman. Petra and Herman have the same father. During different occasions Michael and I had observed that she hardly greets Herman. When asked if she considers Herman her brother, she replied, "No, not really. You see we are not close. We didn't grow up together (*tama kai//are*)" (Interview with Petra, August 2004).

14. Despite the complaints of many elderly Namibians and, as will be seen, also Mexican sisters, in several instances I also observed great affection and tenderness between an older sister and her younger siblings.

15. With Alicia's birth, Pedro, the father, returned to the community.

16. I have translated all Spanish quotations into English.

17. Another woman, Cora, born in 1940 as a middle sister, also highlighted how much her sister closest in age helped her when she menstruated for the first time: "I was shocked. I thought—'What will my mother say?' I started to cry. I was only twelve years old. I cried. Then, my sister, the one close to me, asked me, 'Why do you cry?' I was so ashamed. She said, 'What is it, my dear?' and I said, 'You know, something came out of me.' And she said, 'Do not worry. That has happened to me, too. I will help you'" (Interview with Cora, April 1997).

CHAPTER 3

1. But Adams and Plaut (2003), in a cultural-psychological comparison of ideas and expectations regarding friendship among fifty North-American and fifty Ghanaian respondents, "found" statistically significant differences. North Americans mentioned companionship and emotional support between friends, whereas Ghanaians showed themselves more cautious towards friends and emphasized practical help that friends may offer each other. Caution toward those who are close—"friends" as well as relatives—is widespread in Ghana; it is linked to the fear of evil (jealousy, witchcraft) that those who are close can inflict. Proverbs and inscriptions on cars warning about "friends" and "people in the house" abound (see Field 1960, Van der Geest 2009). That crucial context, which would explain some of Adams's and Plaut's findings, is entirely missing in their article, even though they open their article with a poem expressing exactly this ambivalence towards intimates.

2. This does not contradict observations by several authors that friendship has a low status in society precisely because of its non-formalized position. "Who are you?" someone is asked when he accompanies a friend to the hospital. He has to "admit" that he is not a relative, "just a friend." Lisa M. Tillmann-Healy (2003: 730–31), from whom this example derives, concludes that friendship has a "marginal position within the matrix of interpersonal relations and . . . no clear normative status."

3. Which does not deny that "friendship" is commonly used with instrumental intentions for personal advantage. Friendship in

anthropological fieldwork is a case in point. Both researchers and informants may make statements about friendship to
further their own interests: better research data and social or
material gains, respectively (Bleek 1979). Many years ago, Craig
C. Lundberg (1968) spoke of a "transactional conception of
fieldwork" and Colby R. Hatfield (1973) of "mutual exploitation." Tillmann-Healy (2003), who pleads for friendship as a
method of fieldwork, balances between "true friendship" and
instrumental friendship (which by definition would not qualify
as friendship). Patricia Marshall (2003: 1746), in an article on
ethics in research, writes that researchers should "avoid dupli-
tous 'friend-like' behavior (including acting friendly to get an
interview) performed solely to 'gather' data." See also Wim van
Binsbergen (1979) about the dilemma of instrumental friendship in anthropological fieldwork. Finally, the term *friend* may
also be used in a more general sense, almost as a synonym for
informants one has a good relationship with (as I have been
doing in this very essay).

4. One other study of siblings in Ghana around that same period—
but which falls outside the scope of this article—was a survey
focused on demographic features, in particular the influence of
sex preference on fertility behavior (Addo and Goody 1976).

5. Wolf Bleek was the pseudonym I used to protect the identity of
the family members among whom I did my research (see Van
der Geest 2003). All names of respondents quoted in this essay
are also fictitious.

6. For example, in classic Greek dramas such as *Antigone, Orestes,*
and *Electra*; in Shakespeare's *King Lear, The Taming of the
Shrew, Richard III,* and *As You Like It*; and in Anton Chekhov's
The Three Sisters.

7. For example: Cain and Abel, Jacob and Esau, Joseph and his
brothers, and the parable of the prodigal son. Interestingly,
sister-sister and brother-sister relationships are much less common in both the Old and New Testament.

8. For example: *To Kill a Mockingbird* (Harper Lee), *East of
Eden* (John Steinbeck), *As I Lay Dying* (William Faulkner),
Hotel New Hampshire (John Irving), *Goblin Market* (Christina
Rosetti), *The Agüero Sisters* (Christina Garcia), *Like Water for
Chocolate* (Laura Esquivel), *The Cement Garden* (Ian McEwan),

The Twins (Tessa de Loo), *The Kite Runner* (K. Hosseini), and *The Half-Brother* (Lars Saabye Christensen).

9. For example: *Les enfants terribles* (J. Cocteau), *The Dreamers* (B. Bertolucci), *The Godfather* (F. F. Coppola), *Les Diables* (C. Ruggia), *Scarface* (B. de Palma), *Ani Imouto* (Tadashi Imai), *In Her Shoes* (C. Hanson), and *To the Left of the Father* (L. F. Carvalho).

10. The fifty-seven essays proved problematic "material," as the students presented an unrealistically positive picture of brothers and sisters, probably instigated to do so by the school context where "correct" answers are mandatory. This romanticization of the sibling relationship by students will be the topic of a separate paper and will not be discussed in this essay.

11. Other Akan subgroups include the Asante, Fante, Akyem, Akuapem, Bono, and other smaller groups.

12. Major studies focusing on Kwahu culture and society include Bleek 1975, 1976; Bartle 1977; Miescher 2005; and Crentsil 2006.

13. For a discussion of sibling conflicts over the life course, see also Julia Pauli's contribution in this book.

14. English derogatory term commonly used for a traditional priest (ɔkomfoɔ) or sorcerer (ɔbosomfoɔ, kramo).

15. Today, the tradition of nephews inheriting from their uncles is disappearing.

16. *Dua* means "tree" but also "wood," or anything made of wood. To avoid misunderstanding, no sexual "sleeping" is intended here; sisters sleep with sisters and brothers with brothers. The intimacy and closeness of sharing a bed also is without sexual implications.

17. This text has been taken from a compilation of conversations with six elders about issues of "Life, love and death" (Atuobi et al. 2005). Originally, the conversations were transcribed as they had been held, as dialogues. I have edited those texts in such a way that the questions asked by me have been left out so that the reader only "hears" the elder speak. The meaning of his statements has not been affected by this "intervention."

18. There is a similar quotation in the Gospel of Mark (3:33–35) in which Jesus also transcends the biological meaning of siblinghood:

"Who are my mother and my brothers? . . . Whoever does the will of God is my brother and sister and mother."

19. The absence of sexual connotations in my Kwahu conversations about—and with—brothers and sisters needs further exploration. It is certainly remarkable that incest is widely discussed—perhaps overexposed—in work on brother-sister relations in "Western" societies (see Sabean 2009), while it seems completely absent in the Ghana literature that I have read. Of course, absence in the literature does not prove absence in life. In fact, I asked some of my friends about sexual love between brothers and sisters. The closest I came to brother-sister sexual love were stories of love affairs between cousins that caused great scandal and ended badly.

CHAPTER 4

1. The ethnographic material of this chapter is based on ongoing research in northern Benin since 1992. The quantitative work was done between 1999 and 2004 in three villages in the frame of the research project "Fosterage in Northern Benin" financed by the German research fund.

2. The conflict could be interpreted regarding other themes, as well. For instance, one could focus on the question of children's rights or the fragile boundary between fosterage and bonded labor in Beninois households.

3. For West Africa, see, among others, Clark 1999, Fortes 1949, Goody 1969: 39–90, Piot 1996.

4. Using the term *kinship roles*, I am inspired by the sociological concept of role developed by Ralph Linton (1936) in contrast to structural-functionalist thinking and which I find quite useful, especially in the field of kinship, because it combines elements of structure with agency through individual behavior. Whereas structural-functionalist thinking includes the idea that structure, and here the specific positions in the kinship system (as father, mother, and so on) determine social behavior, the concept of a kinship role stresses the fact that, based on status and the sum of cultural models that include behavior expectations, the concrete action of the person who takes the role is not at all determined. There is space for agency on the part of the actor of the role, in view of the role expectations and the

cultural patterns, on the one hand, and the restrictions caused by the expectations of other kinship roles, on the other. I find it especially useful to think about roles and role expectations in view of the multitude of kinship (and other social) roles a person could and has to play.

5. I take the term *fosterage* here as a general umbrella term that includes different forms of children living with adults other than their biological parents. There were attempts to differentiate the many forms and ways, but as I deal here with changing forms and ways of taking children, I limit myself to using the general term. For a more theoretical discussion, see Alber 2012.

6. In order to protect the identity of my informants, their names have been changed.

7. I use the term *half-brother* here in a widely descriptive sense. As formal and informal polygamy is a common practice among urban and rural Bataombu, children do often have far more siblings with whom they share either the (biological) father or mother than siblings with whom they share both. In Baatonum, no terminological difference between half- and full siblings is made. But there are other expressions of differentiation between both that allow speakers to distinguish.

8. Concerning these institutions and their images about childhood, see Alber 2011 and Howard 2008.

9. Amana tried to respect in public the rule that a biological mother does not have the right to oppose the fosterage of her daughter by the father's sister. This was the reason, only secretly and very carefully, she dared to tell me that she had been completely against the fosterage of her daughter by the aunt, because Djamila had been ready to enter a school career. She told me in a moment when nobody was watching or listening to us.

10. In many rural Baatombu households, boys grow up together as if they were brothers, sharing food, joy, and hardship, even if they are, in kinship terms, uncle and nephew. They would never call themselves brothers, however, since they are always aware of the generational difference, and since correct and informed kinship naming is deeply anchored in norms of Baatombu politeness.

11. Bake's behavior of pushing Kpaasi into the role of Djamila's brother was only possible because in former times, as a pupil,

Kpaasi had also lived for some time in Bake's household (financed by me). Therefore, like me, she acted as Kpaasi's foster mother who has rights over her son. As a good foster son, in both cases, Kpaasi could not completely refuse to do what the mothers asked him to do.

Chapter 5

1. Between 1950 and 1970, China's total fertility rate was around five to six children per woman. After the government started to control childbearing during the 1970s, the rate went down from 5.8 children in 1970 to 2.5 in 1980 (Davis and Harrel 1993: 293).

2. China's unique household registration (户口; *hukou*) system assigns each citizen either agricultural/rural or nonagricultural/ urban status. The percentage of population with rural household registration was 53% in 2010, with an 2.3% annual rate of urbanization estimated for 2010–15 (CIA World Factbook, https://www.cia.gov/library/publications/the-world-factbook/ geos/ch.html, accessed on April 16, 2013).

3. Following early resistance to the "one child only" campaigns in the rural regions, in the mid-1980s family-planning regulations started to allow rural residents to give birth to a second child in case the first one was a girl (Greenhalgh 1993, Greenhalgh and Winckler 2005, Kipnis 2009). For 2009, China's total fertility rate was estimated to be 1.79 (CIA World Factbook, accessed from https:// www.cia.gov/library/publications/the-world-factbook/geos/ ch.html, on October 2, 2011).

4. The contemporary Chinese system is labeled in various ways— for example, "late-socialist," "market-socialist," "post-socialist," or even "post-reform." I prefer *reform-socialist* since, as Chris Hann (2009: 257) has pointed out, this term concurs with the point of view of the majority of the Chinese population, who usually refer to present-day China as *the reform era* but still consider their country to be socialist.

5. I use *generations* here in the sense of a number of age cohorts sharing a particular historical experience. According to Karl Mannheim (1964), different "generational contexts" are defined by rapid political and cultural changes that distinguish them from one another.

6. Field research was conducted from August 2006 until September 2007. Huining County is located in the eastern part of Gansu province, in one of the poorest regions of China. Research in a village was complemented by a survey conducted among 162 students from rural Huining enrolled at two universities in the provincial capital of Lanzhou, as well as interviews with 51 graduates from the region who lived in the Huining county seat in the provincial capital of Lanzhou, or in Beijing.

7. In the planned economy, urban employment in a work unit (单位; *danwei*) guaranteed the "cradle-to-grave" security (Croll 1999: 684) of the so-called iron rice bowl. Social benefits included free housing, medical care, child care, protection from unemployment, and so on.

8. In Chinese kinship terminology, brothers are addressed with respect to their position within the brother set. The serial number according to birth order ("the eldest," "the second," "the third," "the fourth," "the fifth," "the sixth/the little one") precedes the kinship position toward the speaker. Since personal names were hardly used locally, I follow the custom of using ordinal numbers and kinship position instead of personal names.

9. Different from "family management," official representation of the family as the "family head" (家长; *jiazhang*) in the government administrative bodies was assigned according to seniority to the eldest brother in the household—in this case, the third brother. Since the third brother had almost no cash on hand, day-to-day proceedings of the household in terms of consumption were decided by the fifth brother and his wife.

10. The proverb refers to the notion of *zhanguan* (沾光; "to share the light"), which indicates the moral obligation to let others share in the benefits of one's achievement. It relates to a famous folk story about a Daoist man who after years of self-cultivation ascended to the immortal world. All his chicken and dogs flew up with him, shared in his merits, and became immortal as well (Yan 1996: 129).

11. Research included thirty-two cases of graduates born before 1975 who can be classified as "early graduates."

12. According to the revised Marriage Law legislated in 1981, both sons and daughters are equally liable to provide support for their elderly parents. The legal obligation of children to support

their parents has been reconfirmed by the 1996 Law on Protection of the Rights and Interest of the Elderly.

13. I borrow the term *diagonal* from historical demography (for example, Campbell and Lee 2008).

14. For a discussion on the notion of the "quality child," see, for example, Kipnis (2006) and Jacka (2009).

15. In the survey I conducted among students from rural Huining (born in the early 1980s) at two tertiary institutions in Lanzhou, only 6 percent did not have any siblings, 30 percent had one sibling, 41 percent had two siblings, and 20 percent had three siblings (N=162).

16. By the time of field research, the gender ratio at secondary high schools in the region was about sixty/forty (male/female).

CHAPTER 6

1. On the effect of mortality on kin relationships, see Uhlenberg 1980.

2. In 1960–65, women in Ghana had, on average, 6.9 children, while in 2000–2003, 4.4 children (Ghana Statistical Service 2005).

3. All names are pseudonyms.

4. Gracia Clark (1994) notes how traders in Kumasi try to keep their children out of the marketplace, relying on assistance from others in their household, including older children.

5. People in Ayacucho, Peru, put a similar emphasis on poverty as the reason children circulate between households (Leinaweaver 2008).

6. Kwabena is thus very similar to the children of international migrants left behind in Ghana studied by Tetteh (2008).

7. See Adams, Anderson, and Adonu (2004) on issues of jealousy and trust in other key relationships in southern Ghana.

8. Kindergarten teachers are not paid well in Ghana.

References

Aasgaard, Reidar. 2004. *My Beloved Brothers and Sisters! Christian Siblingship in Paul.* London: T&T Clark.

Aboderin, Isabella. 2004. "Decline in Material Family Support for Older People in Urban Ghana, Africa: Understanding Processes and Causes of Change." *Journal of Gerontology* 59B (3): S128–37.

Adams, Glenn, Stephanie L. Anderson, and Joseph K. Adonu. 2004. "The Cultural Grounding of Closeness and Intimacy." In Debra J. Maslak and Arthur Aron, eds. *The Handbook of Closeness and Intimacy*, 321–39. Mahwah, NJ: Lawrence Erlbaum Associates.

Adams, Glenn, Stephanie L. Anderson, Joseph K. Adonu, and V. C. Plaut. 2003. "The Cultural Grounding of Personal Relationship: Friendship in North American and West African Worlds." *Personal Relationships* 10: 335–49.

Adams, Rebecca and Graham Allan, eds. 1998. *Placing Friendship in Context.* Cambridge: Cambridge University Press.

Addo, Nelson O. and Jack R. Goody. 1976. *Siblings in Ghana.* Legon: University of Ghana.

Adeku, J. 1995. "Ghanaians Outside the Country." In K. A. Twum-Baah, J. S. Nabila, and A. F. Aryee, eds. *Migration Research Study in Ghana*, Volume 2: *International Migration*, 1–18. Accra: Ghana Statistical Service.

Adler, Alfred. 1927. "Characteristics of the First, Second, and Third Child." *Children* 3 (May): 14–52.

Alber, Erdmute. 2013. "The Transfer of Belonging: Theories on Child Fostering in West Africa Reviewed." In Erdmute Alber, Jeannett Martin, Catrien Notermans, eds. *Child Fosterage in West Africa: New Perspectives on Theories and Practices.* Leiden: E. J. Brill.

———. 2012. "Schooling or Working? How Family Decision Processes, Children's Agencies and State Policy Influence the Life Paths of Children in Northern Benin." In Gerd Spittler and

Michael Bourdillon, eds. *Children's Work in Africa*, 169–94. Berlin: Lit Verlag Publisher.

———. 2011. "Child Trafficking in West Africa?" In Ana Marta Gonzales, Laurie de Rose, and Florence Oloo, eds. *Frontiers of Globalization: Kinship and Family Structures in West Africa*, 71–92. Trenton: Africa World Press.

———. 2010. "No School without Foster Families in Northern Benin: A Social Historical Approach." In Haldis Haukanes and Tatjana Thelen, eds. *Parenting after the Century of the Child: Travelling Ideals, Institutional Negotiations and Individual Responses*, 57–78. Aldershot: Ashgate.

———. 2004a. "Grandparents as Foster Parents: Transformations in Foster Relations between Grandparents and Grandchildren in Northern Benin." *Africa* 74 (1): 28–46.

———. 2004b. "'The Real Parents Are the Foster Parents': Social Parenthood among the Baatombu in Northern Benin.'" In Fiona Bowie, ed. *Cross-Cultural Approaches to Adoption*, 33–47. London: Routledge.

———. 2003. "Denying Biological Parenthood: Child Fosterage in Northern Benin." *Ethnos* 68 (4): 487–506.

Alber, Erdmute, Bettina Beer, Julia Pauli, and Michael Schnegg, eds. 2010. *Verwandtschaft heute. Positionen, Ergebnisse und Forschungsperspektiven*. Berlin: Reimer.

Alber, Erdmute, Jeannett Martin, and Tabea Häberlein. 2011. "Webs of Kinship im Wandel: Zur Veränderung von Verwandtschaftsbeziehungen in Westafrika." *Afrika Spectrum* 45 (3): 43–67.

Allman, Jean and Victoria Tashjian. 2000. *"I Will Not Eat Stone": A Women's History of Colonial Asante*. Portsmouth: Heinemann.

Ardayfio-Schandorf, Elizabeth and Margaret Amissah. 1996. "Incidence of Child Fostering among School Children in Ghana." In Ardayfio-Schandorf, ed. *The Changing Family in Ghana*, 179–200. Accra: Ghana Universities Press.

Attah-Poku, Agyemang. 1996. *The Socio-Cultural Adjustment Question: The Role of Ghanaian Immigrant Ethnic Associations in America*. Aldershot: Avebury.

Attias-Donfut, Claudine and Martine Segalen. 2007. *Grands-parents: La famille à travers les générations*, 2nd ed. Paris: Odile Jacob.

Atuobi, Patrick, Anthony Obeng Boamah, and Sjaak van der Geest, eds. 2005. *Life, Love and Death: Conversations with Six Elders in Kwahu-Tafo, Ghana*. Amsterdam: Het Spinhuis.

Bai, Limin. 2006. "Graduate Unemployment: Dilemmas and Challenges in China's Movement to Mass Higher Education." *China Quarterly* 185 (March): 128–44.

Bargach, Jamila. 2001. "Personalizing It: Adoption, Bastardy, Kinship and Familiy." In James D. Faubion, ed. *The Ethics of Kinship*, 71–97. Lanham: Rowman and Littlefield.

Barnard, Alan. 1992. *Hunters and Herders of Southern Africa*. Cambridge: Cambridge University Press.

Barth, Frederik. 1971. "Role Dominance and Father-Son Dominance in Middle Eastern Kinship Systems." In Francis L. K. Hsu, ed. *Kinship and Culture*, 87–95. Chicago: Aldine Publishing.

Bartle, Philip. 1977. "Urban Migration and Rural Identity: An Ethnography of a Kwawu Community." PhD diss., University of Ghana, Legon.

Baumann, Gerd. 1995. "Managing a Polyethnic Milieu: Kinship and Interaction in a London Suburb." *Journal of the Royal Anthropological Institute* 1 (4): 725–41.

Becker, Hans A. 1992. "A Pattern of Generations and Its Consequences." In Becker, ed. *Dynamics of Cohort and Generations Research*, 219–48. Amsterdam: Thesis Publishers.

Bell, Sandra and Simon Coleman, eds. 1999. *The Anthropology of Friendship*. Oxford: Berg.

Blackwood, Evelyn. 2005. "Wedding Bell Blues: Marriage, Missing Men, and Matrifocal Follies." *American Ethnologist* 32 (1): 3–19.

Blake, Judith. 1989. *Family Size and Achievement*. Berkeley: University of California Press.

Bledsoe, Caroline and Uche Isiugo-Abaniche. 1989. "Strategies of Child-Fosterage among Mende Grannies in Sierra Leone." In Ron J. Lesthaeghe, ed. *Reproduction and Social Organisation in Sub-Saharan Africa*, 442–74. Berkeley: University of California Press.

Bleek, Wolf [van der Geest, Sjaak]. 1979. "Envy and Inequality in Fieldwork: An Example from Ghana." *Human Organization* 38 (2): 200–205.

———. 1977. "Marriage in Kwahu, Ghana." In Simon Roberts, ed. *Law and the Family in Africa*, 183–204. The Hague: Mouton.

———. 1976. *Sexual Relationships and Birth Control in Ghana: A Case Study of a Rural Town*. Amsterdam: AntropologischSociologisch Centrum.

———. 1975. *Marriage, Inheritance and Witchcraft: A Case Study of a Rural Ghanaian Family*. Leiden: African Studies Centre.

Bloch, Maurice and Dan Sperber. 2004. "Kinship and Evolved Psychological Dispositions: The Mother's Brother Controversy Reconsidered." In Robert Parkin and Linda Stone, eds., *Kinship and Family: An Anthropological Reader*, 438–55. Oxford: Blackwell Publishing.

Bluebond-Langner, Myra. 1991. "Living with Cystic Fibrosis: The Well Sibling's Perspective." *Medical Anthropology Quarterly* 5 (2): 133–52.

Böck, Monika and Aparna Rao, eds. 2000. *Culture, Creation and Procreation. Concepts of Kinship in South Asian Practice*. New York: Berghahn.

Boehm, Deborah. 2011. "Here/Not Here: Contingent Citizenship and Transnational Mexican Children." In Cati Coe, Rachel R. Reynolds, Deborah A. Boehm, Julia Meredith Hess, and Heather Rae-Espinoza, eds. *Everyday Ruptures: Children, Youth, and Migration in Global Perspective*, 161–73. Nashville: Vanderbilt University Press.

Borneman, John. 1996. "Until Death Do Us Part: Marriage/Death in Anthropological Discourse." *American Ethnologist* 23 (2): 215–38.

Brain, Robert. 1977. *Friends and Lovers*. London: Paladin.

Brandtstädter, Susanne. 2003. "The Moral Economy of Kinship and Property in Southern China." In Chris Hann, ed. *The Postsocialist Agrarian Question*, 419–40. Münster: LIT Verlag.

Bryceson, Deborah and Ulla Vuorela, eds. 2002. *The Transnational Family. New European Frontiers and Global Networks*. Oxford: Berg.

Burawoy, Michael. 1998. "The Extended Case Method." *Sociological Theory* 16 (1): 4–33.

Bushin, Naomi. 2011. "Children's Agency in Family Migration Decision Making in Britain." In Cati Coe, Rachel R. Reynolds, Deborah A. Boehm, Julia Meredith Hess, and Heather Rae-Espinoza, eds. *Everyday Ruptures: Children, Youth, and Migration in Global Perspective*, 23–38. Nashville: Vanderbilt University Press.

Campbell, Cameron and James Lee. 2008. "Kin Networks, Marriage, and Social Mobility in Late Imperial China." *Social Science History* 32 (2): 175–214.

Cannell, Fenella and Susie McKinnon. 2013. "Introduction: Vital Relations: Kinship and the Critique of Modernity." In Cannell and McKinnon, eds. *Vital Relations: Kinship and the Critique of Modernity*, 1–24. Santa Fe: School for Advanced Research Press.

Carsten, Janet. 2007. "Introduction: Ghosts of Memory." In Janet Carsten, ed. *Ghosts of Memory: Essays on Remembrance and Relatedness*, 1–35. Malden: Blackwell.

———. 2004. *After Kinship*. Cambridge: Cambridge University Press.

———. 2000. *Cultures of Relatedness: Approaches to the Study of Kinship*. Cambridge: Cambridge University Press.

———. 1997. *The Heat of the Hearth: The Process of Kinship in a Malay Fishing Community*. Oxford: Clarendon Press.

Cepaitiene, Auksuole. 2008. "Wagon Brothers, Wagon Sisters: Symbolic and Actual Siblingship in a Situation of Life Crisis." Paper at EASA Conference, Ljubljana, August.

Clark, Gracia. 1999. "Negotiating Asante Family Survival in Kumasi, Ghana." *Africa* 69 (1): 66–85.

———. 1994. *Onions Are My Husband: Survival and Accumulation by West African Market Women*. Chicago: University of Chicago Press.

Clerkx, Lily. 2009. "Hans und Gretel—About Love between Brothers and Sisters in West-European Fairytales." Unpublished paper.

Coe, Cati. 2012. "Transnational Parenting: Child Fostering in Ghanaian Immigrant Families." In Randy Capps and Michael Fix, eds. *Young Children of Black Immigrants in America: Changing Flows, Changing Faces*. Washington, DC: Migration Policy Institute.

———. 2008. "The Structuring of Feeling in Ghanaian Transnational Families." *City & Society* 20 (2): 222–50.

Cornwall, Andrea. 2005. "Introduction: Perspectives on Gender in Africa." In Cornwall, ed. *Readings in Gender in Africa*, 1–19. Oxford: James Currey.

Crentsil, Perpetual. 2006. *Death, Ancestors and HIV/AIDS among the Akan of Ghana*. Helsinki: Helsinki University Press.

Croll, Elisabeth. 1999. "Social Welfare Reform: Trends and Tensions." *China Quarterly* 159 (September): 684–700.

D'Alisera, JoAnn. 2004. *An Imagined Geography: Sierra Leonean Muslims in America*. Philadelphia: University of Pennsylvania Press.

Davidoff, Leonore. 2012. *Thicker Than Water: Siblings and Their Relations, 1780–1920*. Oxford: Oxford University Press.

———. 2011. "Gender and Age in Nineteenth-Century Britain: The Case of Anne, William, and Helen Gladstone." In Christopher H. Johnson and David Warren Sabean, eds. *Sibling Relations and the Transformations of European Kinship, 1300–1900*, 289–322. New York: Berghahn Books.

Davis, Deborah and Stevan Harrel. 1993. "Introduction." In Deborah Davis and Stevan Harrell, eds. *Chinese Families in the Post-Mao Era*, 1–22. Berkeley: University of California Press.

Delaney, Carol. 2001. "Cutting the Ties that Bind: The Sacrifice of Abraham and Patriarchal Kinship." In Sarah Franklin and Susan McKinnon, eds. *Relative Values: Reconfiguring Kinship Studies*, 413–65. Durham: Duke University Press.

Demian, Melissa. 2004. "Transactions in Rights, Transactions in Children: A View of Adoption from Papua New Guinea." In Fiona Bowie, ed. *Cross-Cultural Approaches to Adoption*, 97–110. London: Routledge.

Dent, Alexander Sebastian. 2007. "Country Brothers: Kinship and Chronotope in Brazilian Rural Popular Culture." *Anthropological Quarterly* 80 (2): 455–95.

Desai, Amit and Evan Killick, eds. 2010. *The Ways of Friendship: Anthropological Perspectives*. Oxford: Berghahn.

Dong, Haiying and Xuehong Wan. 2012. "Higher Education Tuition and Fees in China. Implications and Impacts on Affordability and Educational Equity." *Current Issues in Education* 50 (1). Available at: http://cie.asu.edu/ojs/index.php/cieatasu/article/view/811.

Douglas, Mary. 1971. "Is Matriliny Doomed in Africa?" In Mary Douglas and Phyllis M. Kaberry, eds. *Man in Africa*, 123–37. Garden City: Anchor Books.

Drotbohm, Heike. 2012. "Transnational Motherhood." In Erdmute Alber, Jeannett Martin, and Catrien Notermans, eds. *Fostering in West Africa Reviewed.* Leiden: E. J. Brill.

———. 2009. "Narratives of Equality, Realities of Disparity: Negotiating Siblinghood in Transnational Creole Societies." Paper presented at the conference on Brother- and Sisterhood, University of Bayreuth, November.

Dunn, Judy and Carol Kendrick. 1982. *Siblings: Love, Envy, and Understanding.* Cambridge: Harvard University Press.

Elder, Glen H. and Avshalom Caspi. 1990. "Studying Lives in a Changing Society: Sociological and Personological Explorations." In A. I. Rabin, Robert A. Zucker, Robert A. Emmons, and Susan Frank, eds. *Studying Persons and Lives,* 201–47. New York: Springer.

Empez Vidal, Nuría. 2011. "The Transnationally Affected: Spanish State Policies and the Life-Course Events of Families in North Africa." In Cati Coe, Rachel R. Reynolds, Deborah A. Boehm, Julia Meredith Hess, and Heather Rae-Espinoza, eds. *Everyday Ruptures: Children, Youth, and Migration in Global Perspective,* 174–87. Nashville: Vanderbilt University Press.

Erel, Umut. 2002. "Reconceptualizing Motherhood: Experiences of Migrant Women from Turkey Living in Germany." In Deborah Bryceson and Ulla Vuorela, eds. *The Transnational Family: New European Frontiers and Global Networks,* 127–46. Oxford: Berg.

Errington, Shelly. 1989. *Meaning and Power in a Southeast Asian Realm.* Princeton: Princeton University Press.

Ervin-Tripp, Susan. 1989. "Sisters and Brothers." In Patricia Goldring Zukow, ed. *Sibling Interaction across Cultures: Theoretical and Methodological Issues,* 184–95. New York: Springer-Verlag.

Field, M. J. 1960. *Search for Security: An Ethno Psychiatric Study of Rural Ghana.* London: Faber and Faber.

Fong, Vanessa. 2004. *Only Hope: Coming of Age under China's One-Child Policy.* Stanford: Stanford University Press.

Fortes, Meyer. 1970. *Time and Social Structure and Other Essays.* London: Athlone Press.

———. 1969. *Kinship and the Social Order: The Legacy of Lewis Henry Morgan.* London: Routledge and Kegan Paul.

————. 1949. *The Web of Kinship among the Tallensi: The Second Part of an Analysis of the Social Structure of a Trans-Volta Tribe*. London: Oxford University Press.

Franklin, Sarah and Helena Ragoné, eds. 1998. *Reproducing Reproduction: Kinship, Power, and Technological Innovation*. Philadelphia: University of Pennsylvania Press.

Gamburd, Michele Ruth. 2000. *The Kitchen's Spoon Handle: Transnationalism and Sri Lanka's Migrant Households*. Ithaca: Cornell University Press.

Geissler, Wenzel, Reynolds Whyte, and Erdmute Alber. 2004. *Grandparents and Grandchildren*. Edinburgh: Edinburgh University Press.

Ghana Statistical Service. 2005. "Ghana 2003: Results from the Demographic and Health Survey." *Studies in Family Planning* 36 (2): 158–62.

————. 2002. *2000 Population and Housing Census: Special Report on 20 Largest Localities*. Accra: Ghana Statistical Service.

Gibson, Thomas. 1995. "Having Your House and Eating It: Houses and Siblings in Ara, South Sulawesi." In Janet Carsten and Stephen Hugh-Jones, eds. *About the House: Lévi-Strauss and Beyond*, 129–48. New York: Cambridge University Press.

Gluckman, Max, J. C. Mitchell, and J. A. Barnes. 1949. "The Village Headman in British Central Africa." *Africa* 19 (2): 89–106.

Godelier, Maurice. 1986. *The Making of Great Men: Male Domination and Power among the New Guinea Baruya*. Translated by Rupert Swyer. Cambridge: Cambridge University Press.

Goetting, Ann. 1986. "The Developmental Tasks of Siblingship over the Life Cycle." *Journal of Marriage and Family* 48 (4): 703–14.

Goody, Esther. 1982. *Parenthood and Social Reproduction*. Cambridge: Cambridge University Press.

Goody, Jack. ed. 1969. *The Developmental Cycle in Domestic Groups*. Cambridge: Cambridge University Press.

————. 1959. "The Mother's Brother and the Sister's Son in West Africa." *Journal of the Royal Anthropological Institute* 89: 61–88.

Gottlieb, Alma. 2004. *The Afterlife Is Where We Come From: The Culture of Infancy in West Africa*. Chicago: University of Chicago Press.

Grandits, Hannes. 2010. "Introduction: The Reshaping of Family and Kin Relations in European Welfare." In Hannes Grandits, ed.

Family, Kinship and State in Contemporary Europe, Volume 1: *The Century of Welfare*, 23–46. Frankfurt am Main: Campus.

Grandits, Hannes and Patrick Heady, eds. 2003. *Distinct Inheritances: Property, Family and Community in a Changing Europe*. Münster: LIT.

Greenhalgh, Susan. 1993. "The Peasantization of the One Child Family in Shaanxi." In Deborah Davis and Stevan Harrell, eds. *Chinese Families in the Post-Mao Era*, 219–50. Berkeley: University of California Press.

Greenhalgh, Susan and Edwin Winckler. 2005. *Governing China's Population*. Stanford: Stanford University Press.

Greiner, Clemens. 2011. "Migration, Translocal Networks and Socio-Economic Stratification in Namibia." *Africa* 81 (4): 606–27.

Griffiths, Anne M. O. 1997. *In the Shadow of Marriage: Gender and Justice in an African Community*. Chicago: University of Chicago Press.

Guyer, Jane I. 1994. "Lineal Identities and Lateral Networks: The Logic of Polyandrous Motherhood." In Caroline Bledsoe and Gilles Pison, eds. *Nuptiality in Sub-Saharan Africa*, 231–52. Oxford: Clarendon.

Hann, Chris. 2009. "Embedded Socialism? Land, Labor and Money in Eastern Xinjiang." In Chris Hann and Keith Hart, eds. *Market and Society: The Great Transformation Today*, 256–71. Cambridge: Cambridge University Press.

Hatfield, Colby R. 1973. "Fieldwork: Toward a Model of Mutual Exploitation." *Anthropological Quarterly* 46: 15–29.

Haukanes, Haldis and Tatjana Thelen. 2010. "Parenthood and Childhood: Debates within the Social Sciences." In Thelen and Haldis, eds. *Parenting after the Century of the Child*, 11–32. Burlington: Ashgate.

Hauschild, Thomas. 2008. *Ritual und Gewalt. Ethnologische Studien an europäischen und mediteranen Gesellschaften*. Frankfurt am Main: Suhrkamp.

Herzfeld, Michael. 2007. "Global Kinship: Anthropology and the Politics of Knowing." *Anthropological Quarterly* 80 (2): 313–23.

———. 1997. *Cultural Intimacy: Social Poetics in the Nation State*. New York: Routledge.

Hirsch, Jennifer S. 2003. *A Courtship after Marriage: Sexuality and Love in Mexican Transnational Families*. Berkeley: University of California Press.

Hohkamp, Michaela. 2011. "Do Sisters Have Brothers? The Search for the '*rechte Schwester*': Brothers and Sisters in Aristocratic Society at the Turn of the Sixteenth Century." In Christopher H. Johnson and David Warren Sabean, eds. *Sibling Relations and the Transformations of European Kinship, 1300–1900*, 65–83. New York: Berghahn Books.

Hondagneu-Sotelo, Pierrette. 1994. *Gendered Transitions: Mexican Experiences of Immigration*. Berkeley: University of California Press.

Hondagneu-Sotelo, Pierrette and Ernestine Avila. 1997. "'I'm Here, but I'm There': The Meanings of Latina Transnational Motherhood." *Gender & Society* 11 (5): 548–71.

Howard, Neil. 2008. "Independent Child Migration in Southern Benin: An Ethnographic Challenge to the 'Pathological' Paradigm." Master's thesis, Development Studies, University of Oxford.

Howell, Signe. 2006. *The Kinning of Foreigners: Transnational Adoption in a Global Perspective*. London: Berghahn.

Hsu, Francis L. K. 1971. "A Hypothesis on Kinship and Culture." In Francis L. K. Hsu, ed. *Kinship and Culture*, 3–41. Chicago: Aldine Publishing.

Hüwelmeier, Gertrud. 2009. "Women's Congregations as Transnational Social Security Networks." In Carolin Leutloff-Grandits, Anja Peleikis, and Tatjana Thelen, eds. *Social Security in Religious Networks: Anthropological Perspectives on New Risks and Ambivalences*, 187–205. New York: Berghahn.

Isiugo-Abanihe, Uche Charlie. 1985. "Child Fostering in West Africa." *Population and Development Review* 11 (1): 53–73.

Jacka, Tamara. 2009. "Cultivating Citizens: Suzhi (Quality) Discourse in the PRC." *Positions: East Asia Cultures Critique* 17 (3): 523–35.

Jauch, Herbert M. 1998. *Affirmative Action in Namibia: Redressing the Imbalances of the Past?* Windhoek: New Namibian Books.

Johnson, Christopher H. and David Warren Sabean, eds. 2011. *Sibling Relations and the Transformations of European Kinship, 1300–1900*. New York: Berghahn.

Johnson-Hanks, Jennifer. 2002. "On the Limits of the Life Cycle in Ethnography: Toward a Theory of Vital Conjunctures." *American Anthropologist* 104: 865–80.

Jones, Delmos. 1992. "Which Migrants? Temporary or Permanent?" In Nina Glick Schiller, Linda Basch, and Cristina Blanc-Szanton, eds. *Towards a Transnational Perspective on Migration*, 217–24. New York: New York Academy of Sciences.

Jordan, David K. 1985. "Sworn Brothers: A Study in Chinese Ritual Kinship." In Hsieh Jih-chang and Chuang Ying-Chang, eds. *The Chinese Family and Its Ritual Behavior*, 232–62, 303–4, 310–16. Taipei: Institute of Ethnology, Academia Sinica (Monographic Series B, No. 15).

Joseph, Suad. 1994. "Brother/Sister Relationships: Connectivity, Love, and Power in the Reproduction of Patriarchy in Lebanon." *American Ethnologist* 21 (1): 50–73.

Kapadia, Karin. 1995. *Siva and Her Sisters: Gender, Caste, and Class in Rural South India*. Boulder: Westview Press.

Kaye, Barrington. 1962. *Bringing Up Children in Ghana*. London: Georges Allen and Unwin.

Killick, Evan. 2010. "*Ayompari, Compadre, Amigo*: Forms of Fellowship in Peruvian Amazonia." In Amit Desai and Killick, eds. *The Ways of Friendship: Anthropological Perspectives*, 46–68. Oxford: Berghahn.

Killick, Evan, and Amit Desai. 2010. "Introduction: Valuing Friendship." In Desai and Killick, eds. *The Ways of Friendship: Anthropological Perspectives*, 1–19. Oxford: Berghahn.

Kipnis, Andrew. 2009. "Education and the Governing of Child-Centered Relatedness." In Susanne Brandtstädter and Gonçalo D. Santos, eds. *Chinese Kinship: Contemporary Anthropological Perspectives*, 204–22. London: Routledge.

———. 2006. "Suzhi: A Keyword Approach." *China Quarterly* 186 (June): 195–313.

———. 1997. *Producing Guanxi: Sentiment, Self, and Subculture in a North China Village*. Durham: Duke University Press.

———. 1996. "The Language of Gifts: Managing Guanxi in a North China Village." *Modern China* 22 (3): 285–314.

Kipp, Rita Smith. 1986. "Terms of Endearment: Karo Batak Lovers as Siblings." *American Ethnologist* 13 (4): 632–45.

Kligman, Gail. 1992. "The Politics of Reproduction in Ceaucescu's Romania: A Case Study in Political Culture." *East European Politics and Societies* 6 (3): 364–418.

Kopytoff, Igor. 1971. "The Suku of the Congo: An Ethnographic Test of Hsu's Hypothesis." In Francis L. K. Hsu, ed. *Kinship and Culture*, 69–86. Chicago: Aldine Publishing.

Lamb, Sarah. 2009. *Aging and the Indian Diaspora: Cosmopolitan Families in India and Abroad*. Bloomington: Indiana University Press.

Lambek, Michael. 2011. "Kinship as Gift and Theft: Acts of Succession in Mayotte and Ancient Israel." *American Ethnologist* 38 (1): 2–16.

Lancy, David F. 2008. *The Anthropology of Childhood, Cherubs, Chattel, Changelings*. Cambridge: Cambridge University Press.

Leinaweaver, Jessaca B. 2008. *The Circulation of Children: Kinship, Adoption, and Morality in Andean Peru*. Durham: Duke University Press

Lévi-Strauss, Claude. 1969. *The Elementary Structures of Kinship*. Translated by James Harle Bell, John Richard von Sturmer, and Rodney Needham. Revised ed. Boston: Beacon.

Levitt, Peggy. 2001. *The Transnational Villagers*. Berkeley: University of California Press.

Lindenbaum, Shirley. 1987. "The Mystification of Female Labors." In Jane Fishburne Collier and Sylvia Junko Yanagisako, eds. *Gender and Kinship: Essays towards a Unified Analysis*, 221–43. Stanford: Stanford University Press.

Linton, Ralph. 1936. *The Study of Man*. New York: Allpeton-Century Crofts.

Liu, Xin. 2000. *In One's Own Shadow: An Ethnographic Account of the Condition of Post-Reform Rural China*. Berkeley: University of California Press.

Lundbergh, Craig C. 1968. "The Transactional Conception of Fieldwork." *Human Organization* 27: 45–49.

Mannheim, Karl. 1964. "Das Problem der Generationen." In Mannheim, ed. *Wissenssoziologi*, 509–65. Neuwied: Kut H. Wolf.

Manuh, Takyiwaa. 2006. *An 11th Region of Ghana? Ghanaians Abroad*. Accra: Ghana Academy of Arts and Sciences.

Marré, Diana and Laura Briggs, eds. 2009. *International Adoption: Global Inequalities and the Circulation of Children*. New York: New York University Press.

Marshall, Mac. 1983. "Introduction: Approaches to Siblingship in Oceania." In Marshall, ed. *Siblingship in Oceania: Studies on the Meaning of Kin Relations*. ASAO Monograph No. 8. Lanham: University Press of America

———. 1977. "The Nature of Nurture." *American Ethnologist* 4 (4): 643–62.

Marshall, Patricia A. 2003. "Human Subjects Protections, Institutional Review Boards, and Cultural Anthropological Research." *Anthropological Quarterly* 76 (2): 269–86.

Martin, Jeannett. 2007. "Yakubas neues Leben—Zum Wandel der Kindspflegschaftspraxis bei den ländlichen Fée (Mokollé) in Nordbenin." *Afrika Spectrum* 42: 219–49.

Martinez, Wilton. 1993. "Transnational Fiesta" [film]. Berkeley: Berkeley Media LLC.

Mazzucato, Valentina. 2008. "Transnational Reciprocity: Ghanaian Migrants and the Care of Their Parents Back Home." In Erdmute Alber, Sjaak van der Geest, and Susan Reynolds Whyte, eds. *Generations in Africa*, 91–109. Berlin: Lit Verlag.

McKinley, Robert. 1981. "Cain and Abel on the Malay Peninsula." In Mac Marshall, ed. *Siblingship in Oceania: Studies in the Meaning of Kin Relations*, 335–87. Lanham: University Press of America.

Mead, Margaret. 1972. *Blackberry Winter*. New York: William Morrow.

Meier, Barbara. 1999. "Doglientiri: An Institutionalised Relationship between Women among the Bulsa of Northern Ghana." *Africa* 69 (1): 87–107.

Melhuus, Marit. 1996. "Power, Value, and the Ambiguous Meanings of Gender." In Marit Melhuus and Kristi Anne Stolen, eds. *Machos, Mistresses, Madonnas: Contesting the Power of Latin American Gender Imagery*, 230–59. London: Verso.

Miescher, Stephan F. 2005. *Making Men in Ghana*. Bloomington: Indiana University Press.

Minuchin, Patricia. 1985. "Families and Individual Development: Provocations from the Field of Family Therapy." *Child Development* 56: 289–302.

Mitchell, Juliet. 2003. *Siblings: Sex and Violence*. Malden: Blackwell Publishing.

Müller, Ernst Wilhelm. 1997. "Der Vater in Afrika." In H. Tellenbach, ed. *Vaterbilder in Kulturen Asiens, Afrikas und Ozeaniens*, 92–107. Stuttgart: Kohlhammer.

Niehaus, Isaac. 1994. "Disharmonious Spouses and Harmonious Siblings." *African Studies* 53 (1): 115–35.

Notermans, Catrien. 2004. "Sharing Home, Food, and Bed: Pathways of Grandmotherhood in East Cameroon." *Africa* 74 (1): 6–27.

Nuckolls, Charles W., ed. 1993. *Siblings in South Asia: Brothers and Sisters in Cultural Context*. New York: Guilford Press.

Olwig, Karen Fog. 2007. *Caribbean Journeys: An Ethnography of Migration and Home in Three Family Networks*. Durham: Duke University Press.

———. 1999. "Narratives of the Children Left Behind: Home and Identity in Globalized Caribbean Families." *Journal of Ethnic and Migration Studies* 25 (2): 267–84.

Ong, Aihwa. 1999. *Flexible Citizenship: The Cultural Logic of Transnationality*. Durham: Duke University Press.

Oppong, Christine. 1974. *Marriage among a Matrilineal Elite: A Family Study of Ghanaian Civil Servants*. Cambridge: Cambridge University Press.

Ortner, Sherry B. 1973. "On Key Symbols." *American Anthropologist* 75: 1338–46.

Parreñas, Rhacel Salazar. 2004. *Children of Global Migration: Transnational Families and Gendered Woes*. Stanford: Stanford University Press.

Pauli, Julia. 2012. "Creating Illegitimacy: Negotiating Relations and Reproduction within Christian Contexts in Northwest Namibia." *Journal of Religion in Africa* 42 (4): 408–32.

———. 2008. "A House of One's Own: Gender, Migration and Residence in Rural Mexico." *American Ethnologist* 35 (1): 171–87.

———. 2006. "Kinship as Shared Experience: On Relatedness and Social Survival in Rural Namibia and Elsewhere." Paper presented at the EASA Conference, Bristol, United Kingdom.

———. 2000. *Das geplante Kind: Demographischer, wirtschaftlicher und sozialer Wandel in einer mexikanischen Gemeinde*. Hamburg: Lit.

———. n.d. "Celebrating Distinctions: Marriage, Elites and Reproduction in Rural Namibia." Unpublished Habilitation Manuscript, Institute of Social and Cultural Anthropology, University of Cologne.

Pepler, Debra J., Rona Abramovitch, and Carl Corter. 1981. "Sibling Interaction in the Home: A Longitudinal Study." *Child Development* 52 (4): 1344–47.

Piot, Charles. 1996. "Of Slaves and the Gift: Kabre Sale of Kin during the Era of the Slave Trade." *Journal of African History* 37: 31–49.

Pitt-Rivers, Julian. 1973. "The Kith and the Kin." In Jack Goody, ed. *The Character of Kinship*, 89–105. Cambridge: Cambridge University Press.

Pribilsky, Jason. 2007. *La Chulla Vida: Gender, Migration, and the Family in Andean Ecuador and New York City.* Syracuse: Syracuse University Press.

Rabain-Jamin, Jacqueline, Ashley E. Maynard, and Patricia Greenfield. 2003. "Implications of Sibling Caregiving for Sibling Relations and Teaching Interactions in Two Cultures." *Ethos* 31 (2): 204–31.

Radcliffe-Brown, A. R. 1971. "On Rules of Descent and Interkin Behavior." In Nelson Graburn, ed. *Readings in Kinship and Social Structure*, 87–94. New York: Harper and Row.

———. 1950. "Introduction." In Radcliffe-Brown and Daryll Forde, eds. *African Systems of Kinship and Marriage*, 1–85. London: Oxford University Press.

———. 1924. "The Mother's Brother in South Africa." *South African Journal of Science* 21: 542–55.

Radcliffe-Brown, A. R. and Daryll Forde, eds. 1950. *African Systems of Kinship and Marriage.* Oxford University Press: London.

Rae-Espinoza, Heather. 2011. "The Children of Émigrés in Ecuador: Narratives of Cultural Reproduction and Emotion in Transnational Social Fields." In Cati Coe, Rachel R. Reynolds, Deborah A. Boehm, Julia Meredith Hess, and Rae-Espinoza, eds. *Everyday Ruptures: Children, Youth, and Migration in Global Perspective*, 115–38. Nashville: Vanderbilt University Press.

Ramu, G. N. 2006. *Brothers and Sisters in India: A Study of Urban Adult Siblings.* Toronto: University of Toronto Press.

Rapp, Rayna. 1999. *Testing Women, Testing the Fetus: The Social Impact of Amniocentesis in America.* New York: Routledge.

Reay, Marie. 1975–76. "When a Group of Men Takes a Husband." *Anthropological Forum* 4: 77–96.

Robichaux, David L. 1997. "Residence Rules and Ultimogeniture in Tlaxcala and Mesoamerica." *Ethnology* 36: 149–71.

Rohde, Richard F. 1997. "Nature, Cattle Thieves and Various Other Midnight Robbers: Images of People, Place and Landscape in Damaraland, Namibia." PhD diss., Department of Social Anthropology, University of Edinburgh.

Roth, Claudia. 2013 (forthcoming). "The Strength of Badenya Ties: Siblings and Social Security in Old Age—the Case of Urban Burkina Faso." *American Ethnologist*.

Ruppel, Sophie. 2011. "Subordinates, Patrons, and Most Beloved: Sibling Relationships in Seventeenth-Century German Court Society." In Christopher H. Johnson and David Warren Sabean, eds. *Sibling Relations and the Transformations of European Kinship, 1300–1900*, 85–110. New York: Berghahn Books.

Sabean, David W. 2009. "Brother/Sister Incest Discourses in the West since the Mid 1990s." Paper given at workshop, "Brother- and Sisterhood in Changing and Uncertain Times," Bayreuth University.

Sahlins, Marshall. 2011. "What Kinship Is (Part Two)." *Journal of the Royal Anthropological Institute* 17: 227–42.

———. 2010. "What Kinship Is (Part One)." *Journal of the Royal Anthropological Institute* 17: 2–19.

Sanders, Robert. 2009. *Sibling Relationships: Theory and Issues for Practice*. New York: Palgrave Macmillan.

Sanders, Valerie. 2002. *The Brother-Sister Culture in Nineteenth-Century Literature: From Austen to Woolf.* New York: Palgrave Macmillan.

Saussure, Ferdinand de. 1983. *Course in General Linguistics.* Edited by Charles Bally and Albert Sechehaye. Translated by Roy Harris. London: Duckworth.

Schildkrout, Enid. 1978. "The Roles of Children in Urban Kano." In Jean S. La Fontaine, ed. *Sex and Age as Principles of Social Differentiation*, 109–37. New York: Academic Press.

Schmalzbauer, Leah. 2008. "Family Divided: The Class Formation of Honduran Transnational Families." *Global Networks* 8 (3): 329–46.

Schnegg, Michael. 2007. "Blurred Edges, Open Boundaries: The Long Term Development of the Closed Corporate Peasant Community in Rural Mexico." *Journal of Anthropological Research* 63: 5–32.

———. 2006. "Compadres familiares: Das Verhältnis von compadrazgo und Verwandtschaft in Tlaxcala, Mexiko." *Zeitschrift für Ethnologie* 131: 91–109.

———. 2005. *Das Fiesta Netzwerk. Soziale Organisation einer mexikanischen Gemeinde 1679–2001*. Hamburg: Lit.

Schneider, David M. 1984. *A Critique of the Study of Kinship*. Ann Arbor: University of Michigan Press.

Schwartz, Regina. 1997. *The Curse of Cain: The Violent Legacy of Monotheism*. Chicago: University of Chicago Press.

Small, Cathy. 1997. *Voyages: From Tongan Villages to American Suburbs*. Ithaca: Cornell University Press.

Smith, Daniel Jordan. 2001. "Romance, Parenthood and Gender in a Modern African Society." *Ethnology* 40 (2): 129–51.

Sofue, Takao. 1971. "Some Questions about Hsu's Hypothesis: Seen through Japanese Data." In Francis L. K. Hsu, ed. *Kinship and Culture*, 284–87. Chicago: Aldine Publishing.

Spittler, Gerd. 2001. "Teilnehmende Beobachtung als Dichte Teilnahme." *Zeitschrift für Ethnologie* 126: 1–25

Steelman, Lala Carr and Brian Powell. 1989. "Acquiring Capital for College: The Constraints of Family Configuration." *American Sociological Review* 54 (5): 844–55.

Steelman, Lala Carr, Brian Powell, Regina Werum, and Scott Carter. 2002. "Reconsidering the Effects of Sibling Configuration: Recent Advances and Challenges." *Annual Review of Sociology* 28: 243–69.

Stryker, Rachael. 2010. *The Road to Evergreen: Adoption, Attachment Therapy, and the Promise of Family*. Ithaca: Cornell University Press.

Suárez-Orozco, Carola, Irina L. G. Todorova, and Josephine Louie. 2002. "Making Up for Lost Time: The Experience of Separation and Reunification among Immigrant Families." *Family Process* 41 (4): 625–43.

Sutton-Smith, Brian and B. G. Rosenberg. 1970. *The Sibling*. New York: Holt, Reinhart and Winston.

Tetteh, Ernestina. 2008. "Voices of Left Behind Children: A Study of International Families in Accra, Ghana." Master's thesis, University of Ghana, Legon.

Thelen, Tatjana. 2010. "*Kinning* im Alter: Verbundenheit und Sorgebeziehungen ostdeutscher Senior/Innen." In Erdmute Alber,

Bettina Beer, Julia Pauli, and Michael Schnegg, eds. *Verwandtschaft heute*, 225–48. Berlin: Reimer.

———. 2005. "Caring Grandfathers: Changes in Support between Generations in East Germany." In Haldis Haukanes and Frances Pine, eds. *Generations, Kinship and Care: Gendered Provisions of Social Security in Central Eastern Europe*, 163–88. Bergen: University of Bergen.

Thelen, Tatjana, and Haldis Haukanes, eds. 2010. *Parenting after the Century of the Child: Travelling Ideas, Institutional Negotiations and Individual Responses*. Aldershot: Ashgate.

Thelen, Tatjana, and Carolin Leutloff-Grandits. 2010. "Self Sacrifice or Natural Donation? A Life Course Perspective on Grandmothering in New Zagreb (Croatia) and East Berlin (Germany)." *Horizontes Antropologicos* 34: 427–52.

Tillmann-Healy, Lisa. 2003. "Friendship as Method." *Qualitative Inquiry* 9 (5): 729–49.

Trawick, Margaret. 1990. *Notes on Love in a Tamil Family*. Berkeley: University of California Press.

Twum-Baah, K. A. 2005. "Volume and Characteristics of International Ghanaian Migration." In Takyiwaa Manuh, ed. *At Home in the World? International Migration and Development in Contemporary Ghana and West Africa*, 55–77. Accra: Sub-Saharan Publishers.

Van Binsbergen, Wim M. J. 1979. "Anthropological Fieldwork: There and Back Again." *Human Organization* 38 (2): 205–9.

Van der Geest, Sjaak. 2009. "'Anyway!': Lorry Inscriptions in Ghana." In J.-B. Gewald, S. Luning, and K. van Walraven, eds. *The Speed of Change: Motor Vehicles and People in Africa, 1890–2000*, 253–93. Leiden: E. J. Brill.

———. 2003. "Confidentiality and Pseudonyms: A Fieldwork Dilemma from Ghana." *Anthropology Today* 19 (1): 14–18.

Van Velzen, Jaap. 1967. "The Extended Case Method and Situational Analysis." In A. L. Epstein, ed. *The Craft of Social Anthropology*, 129–49. London: Tavistock.

Van Vleet, Krista E. 2008. *Performing Kinship: Narrative, Gender, and the Intimacies of Power in the Andes*. Austin: University of Texas Press.

Weiner, Annette. 1992. *Inalienable Possessions: The Paradox of Keeping-While-Giving*. Berkeley: University of California Press.

Weismantel, Mary. 1995. "Making Kin: Kinship Theory and Zumbagua Adoptions." *American Ethnologist* 22 (4): 685–704.

Weisner, Thomas S. 1993. "Overview: Sibling Similarity and Difference in Different Cultures." In Charles W. Nuckolls, ed. *Siblings in South Asia: Brothers and Sisters in Cultural Context*, 1–18. New York: Guilford Press.

———. 1982. "Sibling Interdependence and Child Caretaking: A Cross-Cultural View." In Michael E. Lamb and Brian Sutton-Smith, eds. *Sibling Relationships: Their Nature and Significance across the Lifespan*, 305–28. Hillsdale: Lawrence Erlbaum Associates.

Weisner, Thomas S. and Ronald Gallimore. 1977. "My Brother's Keeper: Child and Sibling Caretaking." *Current Anthropology* 18 (2): 169–90.

Weston, Kath. 1991. *Families We Choose: Lesbians, Gays, Kinship*. New York: Columbia University Press.

Whyte, Susan Reynolds, Erdmute Alber, and Sjaak van der Geest. 2008. "Generational Connections and Conflicts in Africa: An Introduction." In Alber, van der Geest, and White, eds. *Generations in Africa: Connections and Conflicts*, 1–23. Berlin: Lit Verlag.

Yan, Yunxiang. 2009. *The Individualization of Chinese Society*. Oxford: Berg.

———. 2005. "The Individual and Transformation of Bridewealth in Rural Northern China." *The Journal of the Royal Anthropological Institute* 11 (4): 637–58.

———. 2003. *Private Life under Socialism: Love, Intimacy, and Family Change in a Chinese Village, 1949–1999*. Stanford: Stanford University Press.

———. 1996. *The Flow of Gifts: Reciprocity and Social Networks in a Chinese Village*. Stanford: Stanford University Press.

Yang, Lien-Sheng. 1957. "The Concept of Pao as a Basis for Social Relations in China." In John K. Fairbank, ed. *Chinese Thought and Institutions*, 291–309. Chicago: University of Chicago Press.

Yang, Mayfair Mei-Hui. 1994. *Gifts, Favors, and Banquets: The Art of Social Relationships in China*. Ithaca: Cornell University Press.

Yngvesson, Barbara. 2010. *Belonging in an Adopted World: Race, Identity and Transnational Adoption*. Chicago: University of Chicago Press.

Yoshikawa, Hirokazu. 2011. *Immigrants Raising Citizens: Undocumented Parents and Their Young Children.* New York: Russell Sage Foundation.

Zukow, Patricia Goldring, ed. 1989. *Sibling Interaction across Cultures: Theoretical and Methodological Issues.* New York: Springer-Verlag.

Index

Printed in the United States of America